EASY PICKINGS

PAUL SIMON™

AMSCO PUBLICATIONS
part of The Music Sales Group
New York / London / Paris / Sydney / Copenhagen / Berlin / Madrid / Tokyo

Exclusive Distributors:
MUSIC SALES CORPORATION
257 Park Avenue South
New York, NY 10010, USA
MUSIC SALES LIMITED
Distribution Centre, Newmarket Road,
Bury St Edmunds, Suffolk IP33 3YB, England
MUSIC SALES PTY LIMITED
20 Resolution Drive
Caringbah, NSW 2229, Australia

Order No. PS11600
ISBN 978-0-8256-3641-7

Music edited by Tom Farncombe
Music arranged by David Weston
Music processed by Paul Ewers Music Design
Cover design by Fresh Lemon
Cover illustration courtesy iStockphoto
Interior photos courtesy iStockphoto and LFI
Printed in the United States of America

WELCOME TO EASY PICKINGS™!

EASY PICKINGS™ is the new way to play classic songs in the fingerpicking style. The music in this book doesn't use standard notation. Instead, a simple system shows the guitar strings.

Chord boxes show you where to place your fingers with your fretting hand; crosses on the strings show you the pattern to pick the strings. That's all there is to it!

All the songs in this book have been specially arranged in the EASY PICKINGS™ format to make them as easy as possible. The first few songs have only a few chords, and simple picking patterns; later in the book the songs have more chords and a greater variety of fingerpicking styles. Some of the songs have been arranged in a different key from the original recording. Where this is the case, you'll need a capo, at the fret indicated at the top of the song, to play along.

The pictures below show you all you need to know!

Many of the songs have hints on how to play at the top of the page.

CHORD BOXES

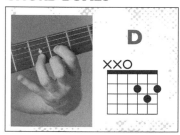

Chord box for a D chord.

Chord boxes are diagrams of the guitar neck viewed head upwards, face on.
They show where to place your fingers to play each chord. Each time you see a new chord box, change to the new chord.

The top line is the nut, the others are the frets. The vertical lines are the strings, starting from E (or 6th) on the left to E (or 1st) on the right.

The black dots indicate where to place your fingers. Strings marked with an O are played open, not fretted; strings marked with an X should not be played. You won't always pick every note of every chord shape that you finger, but it is important to hold each chord in full to learn properly.

 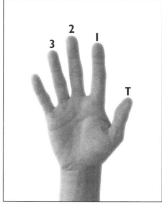

FINGERPICKING

At the start of each song, you'll see the guitar headstock and the strings of the guitar, viewed as if you were playing. The crosses on the strings show each note to be picked with your picking hand.

Usually, you'll play the first note of each group of four with your thumb (T), and the other notes with your 1st (1), 2nd (2) and 3rd (3) fingers. This is shown above some of the patterns as a guide. Follow these fingerings and you'll be playing all the fingerpicking patterns in this book in no time!

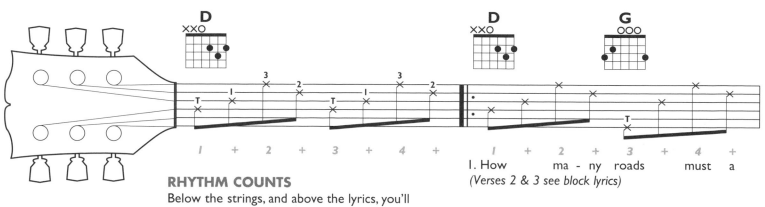

RHYTHM COUNTS

Below the strings, and above the lyrics, you'll see beat counts to keep the rhythm steady.
Each number (or +) is a note to pick.

1. How ma - ny roads must a
(Verses 2 & 3 see block lyrics)

SCARBOROUGH FAIR/CANTICLE
ARRANGEMENT AND ORIGINAL COUNTERMELODY BY
PAUL SIMON AND ARTHUR GARFUNKEL

This song uses four chord shapes: **Em**, **G**, **D** and **A** (shown below), and has an even picking rhythm throughout. Use your thumb to pick the first note of each group of six, and then your 1st, 2nd and 3rd fingers to pick the other five. Play the top three strings with your fingers and pick the lower strings with your thumb for all of the chords in this song.

You'll notice that each bar contains six notes to pick: count '1 + 2 + 3 +' as you play to keep the rhythm steady.

These signs – ‖: :‖ – show that the music repeats for each verse. Play the four verses through; on the first four times, play the bar under the [1–4.] bracket. On the last time through – repeating the first verse – play the final four bars (under the [5.] bracket) instead. The final bar has one chord, which should be picked and allowed to ring rather than picking each note in turn.

Simon and Garfunkel's 1966 folk-rock classic.

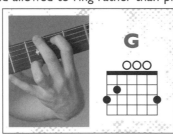
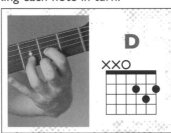
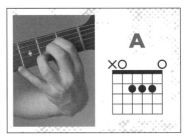

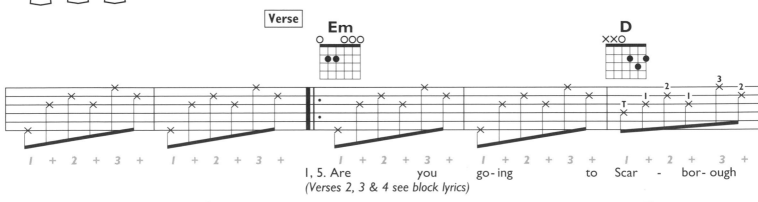

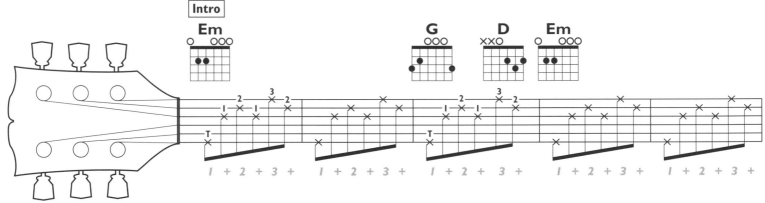

I, 5. Are   you   go - ing   to   Scar - bor- ough
(Verses 2, 3 & 4 see block lyrics)

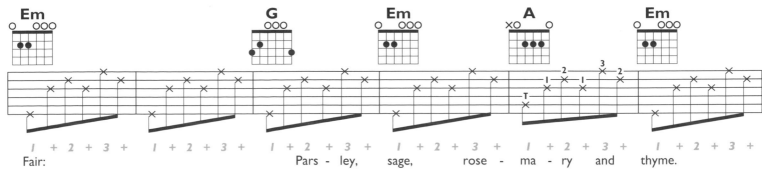

Fair: Pars - ley,   sage,   rose - ma - ry   and   thyme.

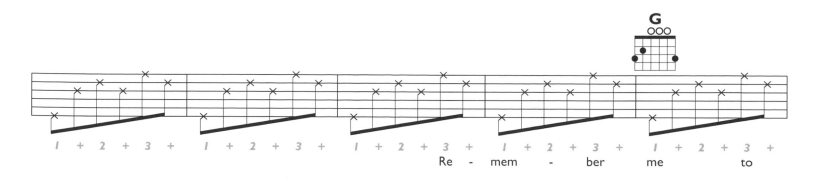

G

| 1 + 2 + 3 + | 1 + 2 + 3 + | 1 + 2 + 3 + | 1 + 2 + 3 + | 1 + 2 + 3 + |

Re - mem - ber me to

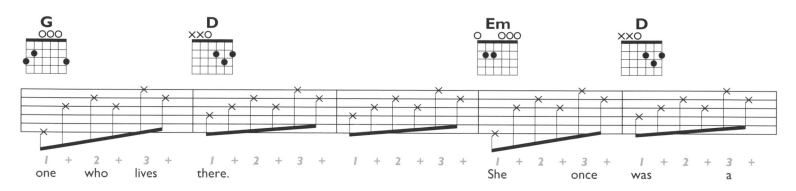

G   **D**   **Em**   **D**

| 1 + 2 + 3 + | 1 + 2 + 3 + | 1 + 2 + 3 + | 1 + 2 + 3 + | 1 + 2 + 3 + |

one who lives there.   She once was a

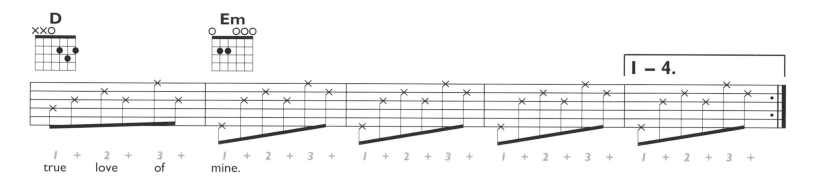

D   **Em**   **1 – 4.**

| 1 + 2 + 3 + | 1 + 2 + 3 + | 1 + 2 + 3 + | 1 + 2 + 3 + | 1 + 2 + 3 + |

true love of mine.

5.   **G**   **D**   **Em**

(Let chord ring)

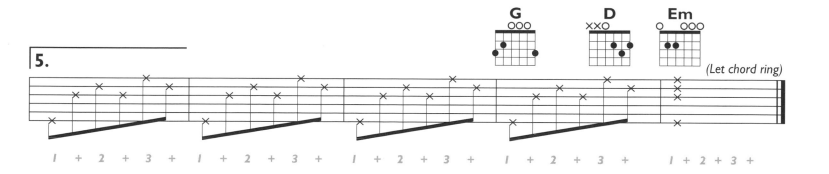

| 1 + 2 + 3 + | 1 + 2 + 3 + | 1 + 2 + 3 + | 1 + 2 + 3 + | 1 + 2 + 3 + |

Verse 2:
Tell her to make me a cambric shirt:
    On the side of a hill in the deep forest green,
Parsley, sage, rosemary and thyme.
    Tracing of sparrow on snow-crested brown.
Without no seams nor needle work,
    Blankets and bedclothes the child of the mountain,
Then she'll be a true love of mine.
    Sleeps unaware of the clarion call.

Verse 3:
Tell her to find me an acre of land:
    On the side of a hill a sprinkling of leaves,
Parsley, sage, rosemary and thyme.
    Washes the grave with silvery tears.
Between the salt water and the sea strand,
    A soldier cleans and polishes a gun.
Then she'll be a true love of mine.

Verse 4:
Tell her to reap it with a sickle of leather:
    War bellows blazing in scarlet battalions,
Parsley, sage, rosemary and thyme;
    Generals order their soldiers to kill.
And gather it all in a bunch of heather,
    And fight for a cause they've long ago forgotten.
Then she'll be a true love of mine.

DUNCAN

WORDS AND MUSIC BY PAUL SIMON

This song uses three main picking patterns – look carefully at the fingerings shown. You always play the top three strings with your fingers, and the lower strings with your thumb, but the pattern changes for certain parts (e.g., the first time you play a **D** chord).

In the **Instrumental** sections after each verse the picking pattern starts with two notes picked together. Play these notes with your thumb and third finger, as shown in the photos below.

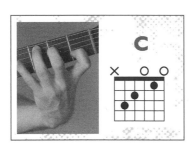

Playing two notes at once.

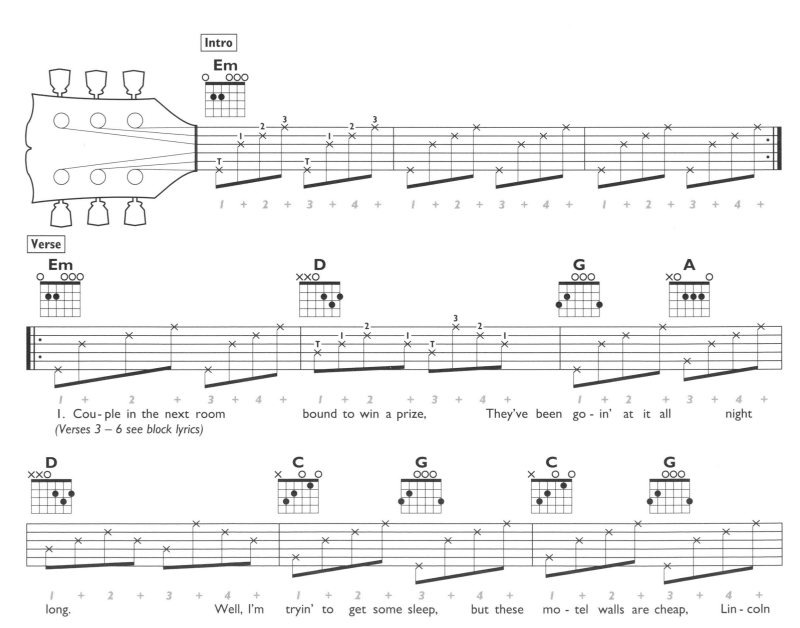

1. Cou - ple in the next room   bound to win a prize,   They've been go - in' at it all   night

(Verses 3 – 6 see block lyrics)

long.   Well, I'm   tryin' to   get some sleep,   but these   mo - tel walls are cheap,   Lin - coln

6

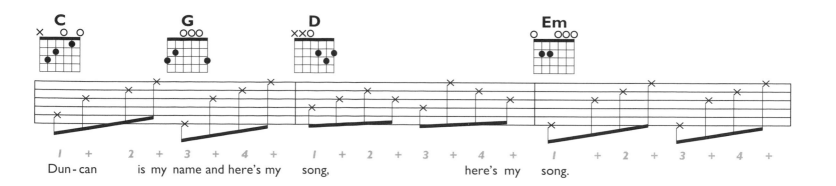

C   G   D   Em

| 1 | + | 2 | + | 3 | + | 4 | + | 1 | + | 2 | + | 3 | + | 4 | + | 1 | + | 2 | + | 3 | + | 4 | + |

Dun - can   is my name and here's my   song,   here's my   song.

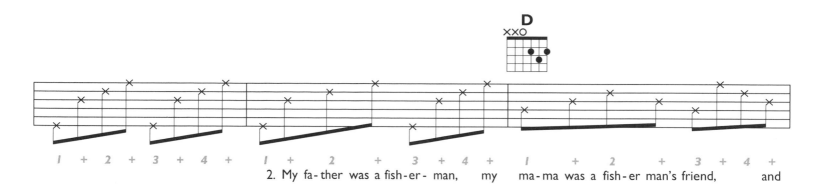

D

| 1 | + | 2 | + | 3 | + | 4 | + | 1 | + | 2 | + | 3 | + | 4 | + | 1 | + | 2 | + | 3 | + | 4 | + |

2. My fa - ther was a fish - er - man,   my   ma - ma was a fish - er man's friend,   and

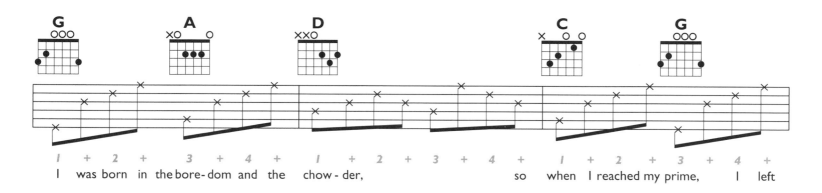

G   A   D   C   G

| 1 | + | 2 | + | 3 | + | 4 | + | 1 | + | 2 | + | 3 | + | 4 | + | 1 | + | 2 | + | 3 | + | 4 | + |

I   was born in the bore - dom and the   chow - der,   so   when I reached my prime,   I   left

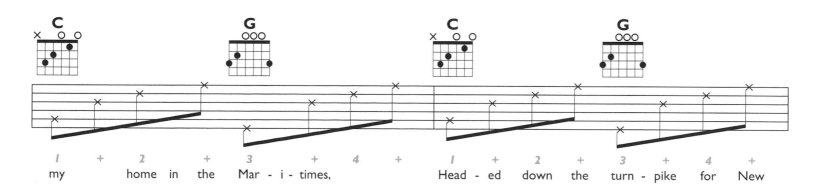

C   G   C   G

| 1 | + | 2 | + | 3 | + | 4 | + | 1 | + | 2 | + | 3 | + | 4 | + |

my   home in the   Mar - i - times,   Head - ed down the   turn - pike for New

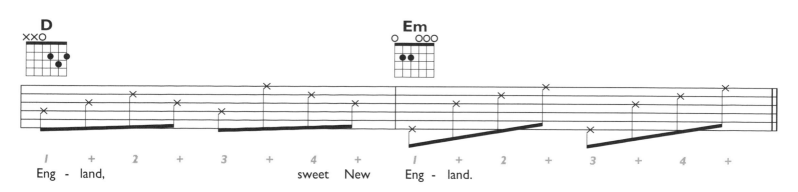

D   Em

| 1 | + | 2 | + | 3 | + | 4 | + | 1 | + | 2 | + | 3 | + | 4 | + |

Eng - land,   sweet New   Eng - land.

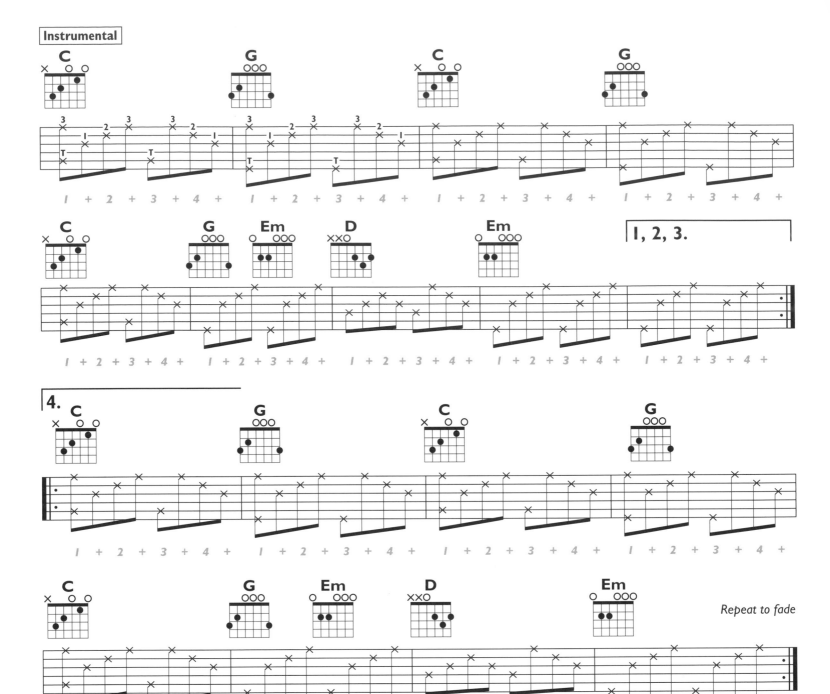

Verse 3:
Holes in my confidence, holes in the knees of my jeans,
I's left without a penny in my pocket,
Oo hoo hoo wee I's about destituted as a kid could be.
And I wished I wore a ring so I could hock it, I'd like to hock it.

Verse 4:
A young girl in the parking lot was preachin' to a crowd
Singin' sacred songs and reading from the Bible,
Well I told her I was lost, and she told me all about the Pentecost,
And I seen that girl as the road to my survival.

Verse 5:
Just later that very same night when I crept to her tent with a flashlight
And my long years of innocence ended,
Well she took me to the woods, sayin'
"Here comes something and it feels so good!"
And just like a dog I was befriended, I was befriended.

Verse 6:
Oh, oh what a night, oh, what a garden of delight,
Even now that sweet memory lingers,
I was playin' my guitar, lying underneath the stars,
Just thankin' the Lord for my fingers, for my fingers.

MOTHER AND CHILD REUNION
WORDS AND MUSIC BY PAUL SIMON

The chords for this song are **G**, **Em**, **C**, **D** and **Am**. Three picking patterns are used, always with your thumb on the lower three strings and your fingers on the top three.

Paul Simon in 1972.

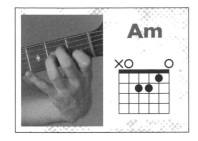

Am

CAPO: 2ND FRET

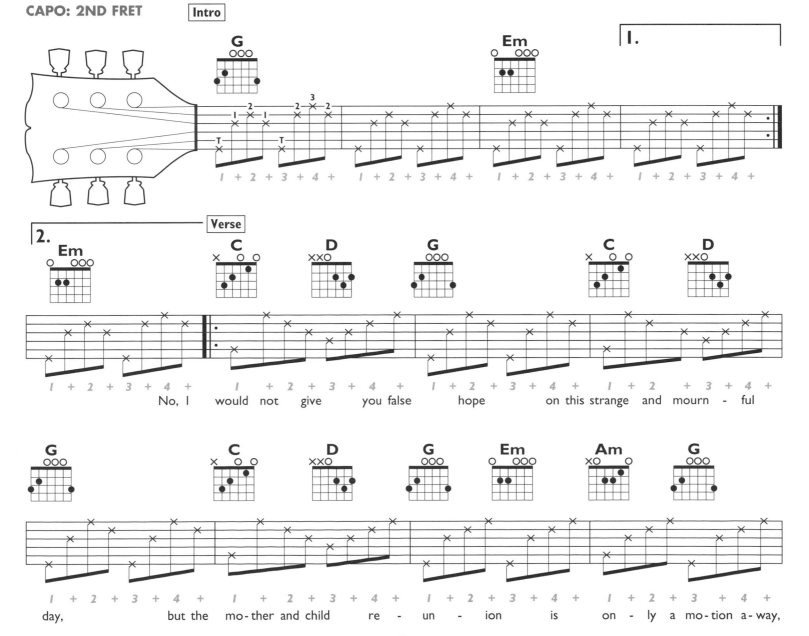

No, I would not give you false hope on this strange and mourn-ful day, but the mo-ther and child re-un-ion is on-ly a motion a-way,

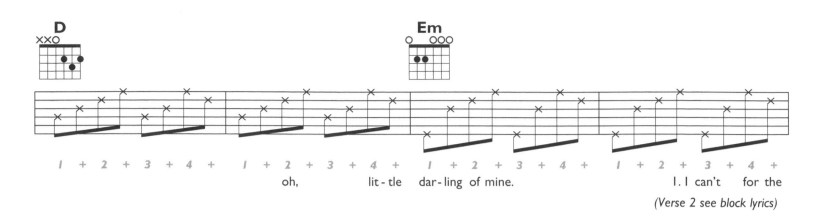

oh,   lit - tle   dar - ling of mine.   1. I can't   for the
(Verse 2 see block lyrics)

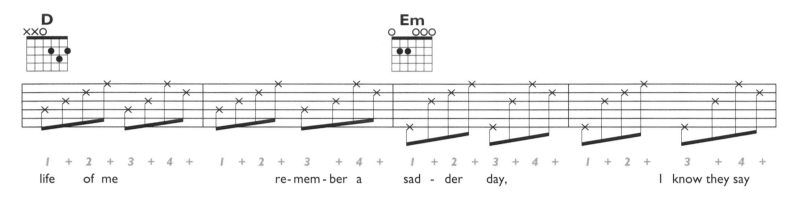

life   of me   re - mem - ber a   sad - der   day,   I know they say

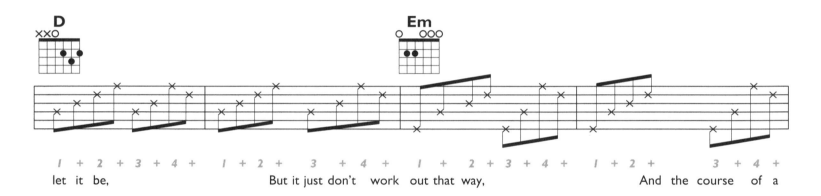

let it be,   But it just don't   work   out that way,   And the course of a

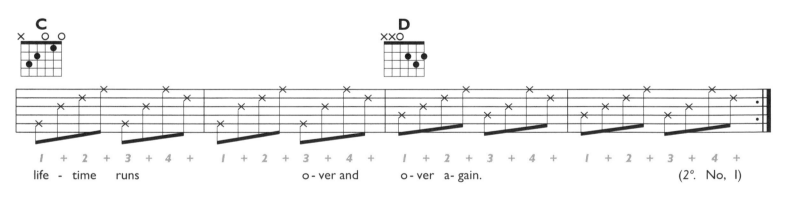

life - time runs   o - ver and   o - ver a - gain.   (2°. No, I)

Chorus

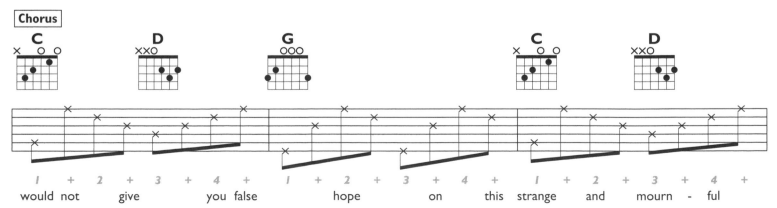

would not   give   you false   hope   on   this strange   and   mourn - ful

Verse 2:
I just can't believe it's so,
and though it seems strange to say,
I never been laid so low
In such a mysterious way.
And the course of as lifetime runs
Over and over again.

11

THE SOUND OF SILENCE
WORDS AND MUSIC BY PAUL SIMON

The **B**♭ chord in this song is a 'barre' shape using the middle four strings of the guitar; barre with your 3rd finger as shown in the photo below. For most of the song, you'll pick the top three strings with your fingers. However, for this **B**♭ chord, move your hand position to pick the 2nd, 3rd and 4th strings instead.

You'll notice that each bar contains eight notes to pick – with the exception of the second bar on the last line of music. This bar just has four notes; count '*1 + 2 +*', and then start the next bar on '*1*'.

Some of the bars in this song use the ⟋ symbol. This means that the pattern in the previous bar is to be repeated exactly.

This song was written following the assassination of President John F. Kennedy on 22 November 1963, capturing the mood of a nation in mourning.

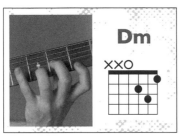

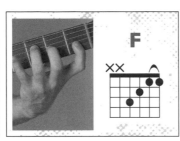

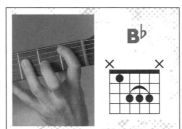

CAPO: 1ST FRET

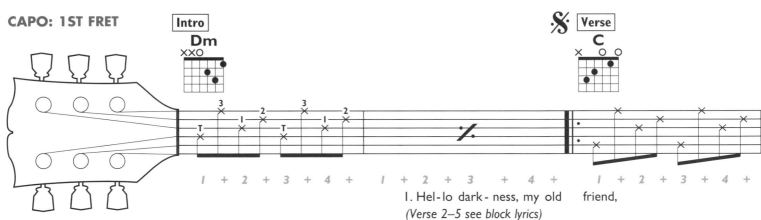

1. Hel-lo dark-ness, my old   friend,
(Verse 2–5 see block lyrics)

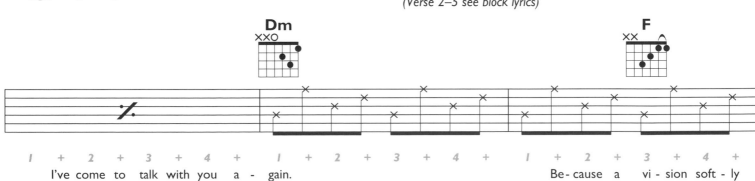

I've come to   talk with you a - gain.   Be-cause a   vi - sion soft - ly

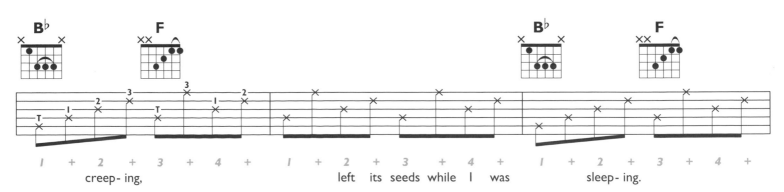

creep- ing,   left   its seeds while I   was   sleep- ing.

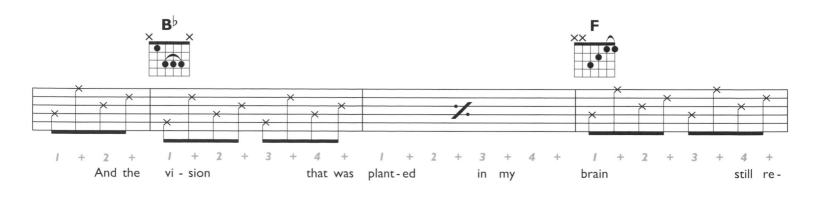

I + 2 + I + 2 + 3 + 4 + I + 2 + 3 + 4 + I + 2 + 3 + 4 +

And the   vi - sion   that was   plant - ed   in my   brain   still re-

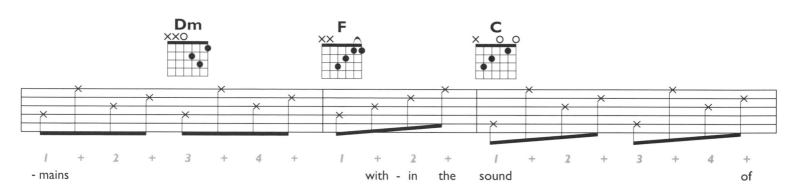

I + 2 + 3 + 4 + I + 2 + I + 2 + 3 + 4 +

- mains   with - in   the   sound   of

I – 4.   **5.**

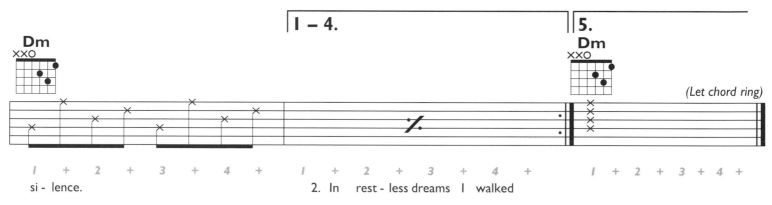

(Let chord ring)

I + 2 + 3 + 4 + I + 2 + 3 + 4 + I + 2 + 3 + 4 +

si - lence.   2. In   rest - less dreams I walked

Verse 2:
In restless dreams I walked alone
Narrow streets of cobblestone,
'Neath the halo of a street lamp,
I turned my collar to the cold and damp
When my eyes were stabbed by the flash of a neon light
That split the night
And touched the sound of silence.

Verse 3:
And in the naked light I saw
Ten thousand people, maybe more.
People talking without speaking,
People hearing without listening,
People writing songs that voices never share
And no one dared
Disturb the sound of silence.

Verse 4:
"Fools" said I, "You do not know
Silence like a cancer grows.
Hear my words that I might teach you,
Take my arms that I might reach you."
But my words like silent raindrops fell,
And echoed in the wells of silence.

Verse 5:
And the people bowed and prayed
To the neon god they made.
And the sign flashed out its warning,
In the words that it was forming.
And the signs said, The words of the prophets
Are written on the subway walls
And tenement halls.
And whisper'd in the sounds of silence.

A HAZY SHADE OF WINTER
WORDS AND MUSIC BY PAUL SIMON

The picking patterns for this song – for instance, in the first four bars – require you to move between picking the top three strings and the 2nd, 3rd and 4th strings with your fingers. Look carefully at the fingerings shown, and these changes will fall into place with practice.

Later in the song is a section where the patterns start with two notes picked together using the thumb and 3rd finger. This is shown in the photo below.

This song featured on Bookends, released in 1968.

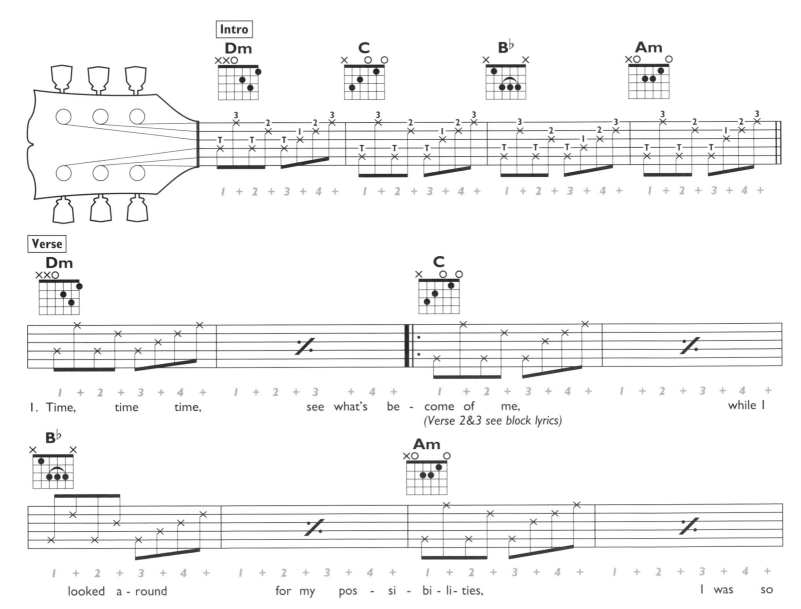

1. Time, time time, see what's be - come of me, while I
(Verse 2&3 see block lyrics)

looked a - round for my pos - si - bi - li - ties, I was so

14

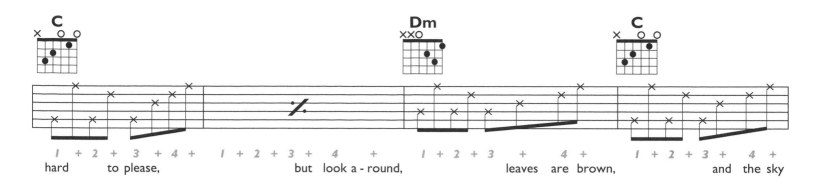

hard   to please,   but look a - round,   leaves are brown,   and the sky

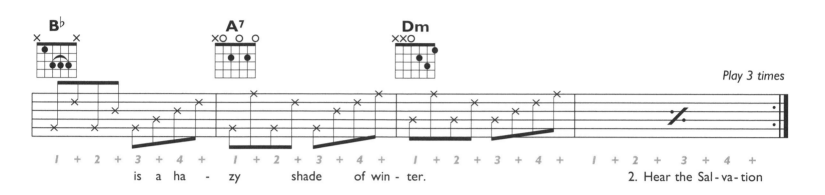

Play 3 times

is a ha - zy   shade   of win - ter.   2. Hear the Sal - va - tion

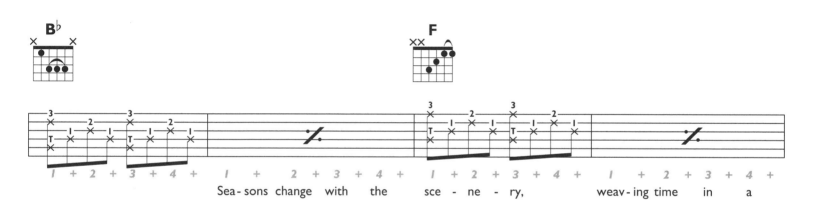

Sea - sons change with   the   sce - ne - ry,   weav - ing time   in a

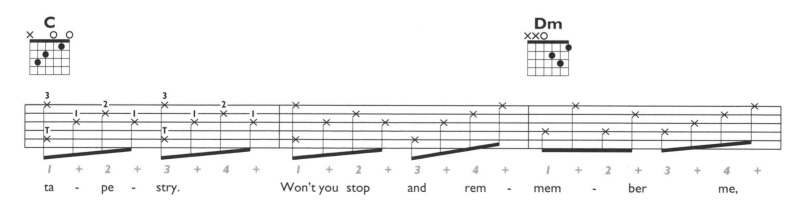

ta - pe - stry.   Won't you stop   and   rem - mem - ber   me,

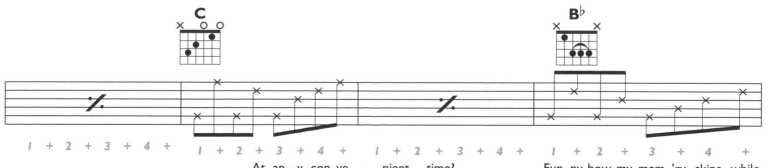

At an - y con - ve - nient time?   Fun - ny how my mem -'ry skips, while

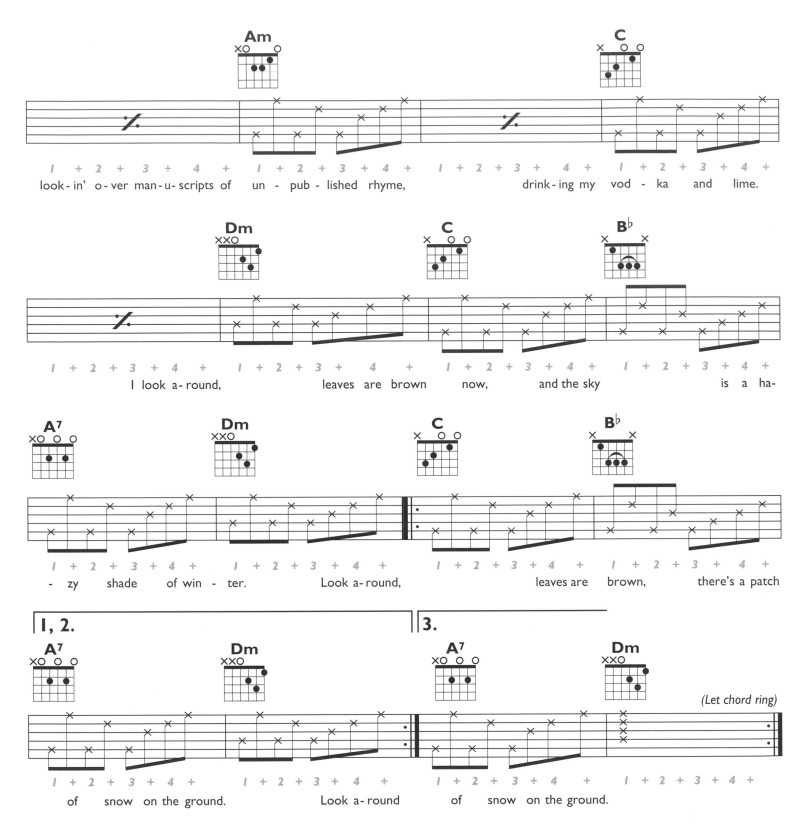

Verse 2:
Hear the Salvation Army Band,
Down by the river side,
It's bound to be a better ride than what you've got planned,
Carry your cup in your hand, and look around,
Leaves are brown now, and the sky is a hazy shade of winter.

Verse 3:
Hang onto your hopes my friend,
That's an easy thing to say,
but if your hopes should pass away,
simply pretend that you can build them again.
Look around, the grass is high, the fields are ripe:
It's the spring time of my life.

Verse 4:
Seasons change with the scenery,
weaving time in a tapestry.
Won't you stop and remember me,
At any convenient time?
Funny how my mem'ry skips,
while lookin' over manuscripts of unpublished rhyme,
drinking my vodka and lime.
I look around, leaves are brown now,
And the sky is a hazy shade of winter.

Look around, leaves are brown, there's a patch of snow on the ground.

TAKE ME TO THE MARDI GRAS
WORDS AND MUSIC BY PAUL SIMON

For this song, most of the picking with your fingers is on the 2nd, 3rd and 4th strings. There are also sections where two notes are picked together (see photo below). Look out for the fingerings shown for these patterns.

The chords for this song include **Bm**. This is a barre chord shape; the curved line in the chord box shows that you 'barre' the strings with your first finger. Compare the sound of the **A⁷** chord with the 'normal' **A** chord.

Some of the bars in this song have no chord box shown, and are marked '**N.C.**' instead. This stands for 'No Chord', and means you play nothing at all!

Paul Simon's 1973 album used a variety of musical styles, including Dixieland Jazz for this song.

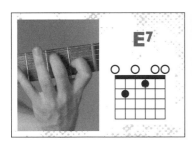

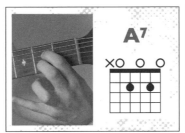

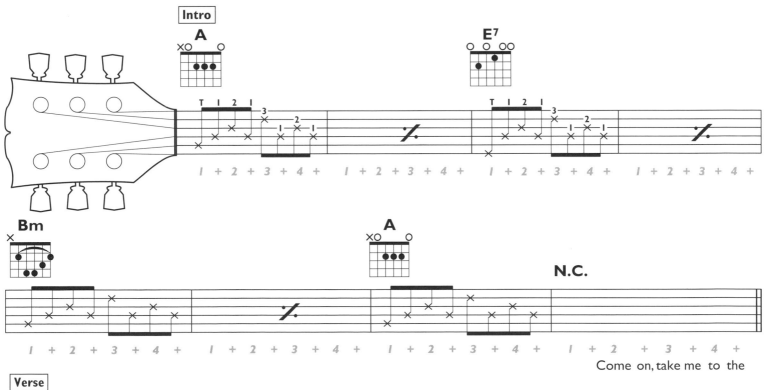

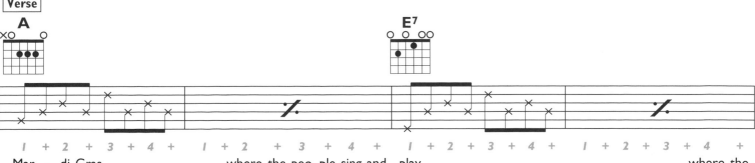

Come on, take me to the

Mar - di Gras   where the peo - ple sing and   play,   where the

dan-cing is e-lite   and there's   mu-sic in the street both night and   day.   Hur-ry, take me to the

Mardi   Gras,   In the ci-ty of my   dreams,   you can

le-gal-ize your laws,   you can   wear you summer clothes in the New Or-leans.

And I will lay my bur-den   down,

Rest my head up-on that shore,   And when I wear that star-ry crown,

I won't be want-ing an-y   more.

18

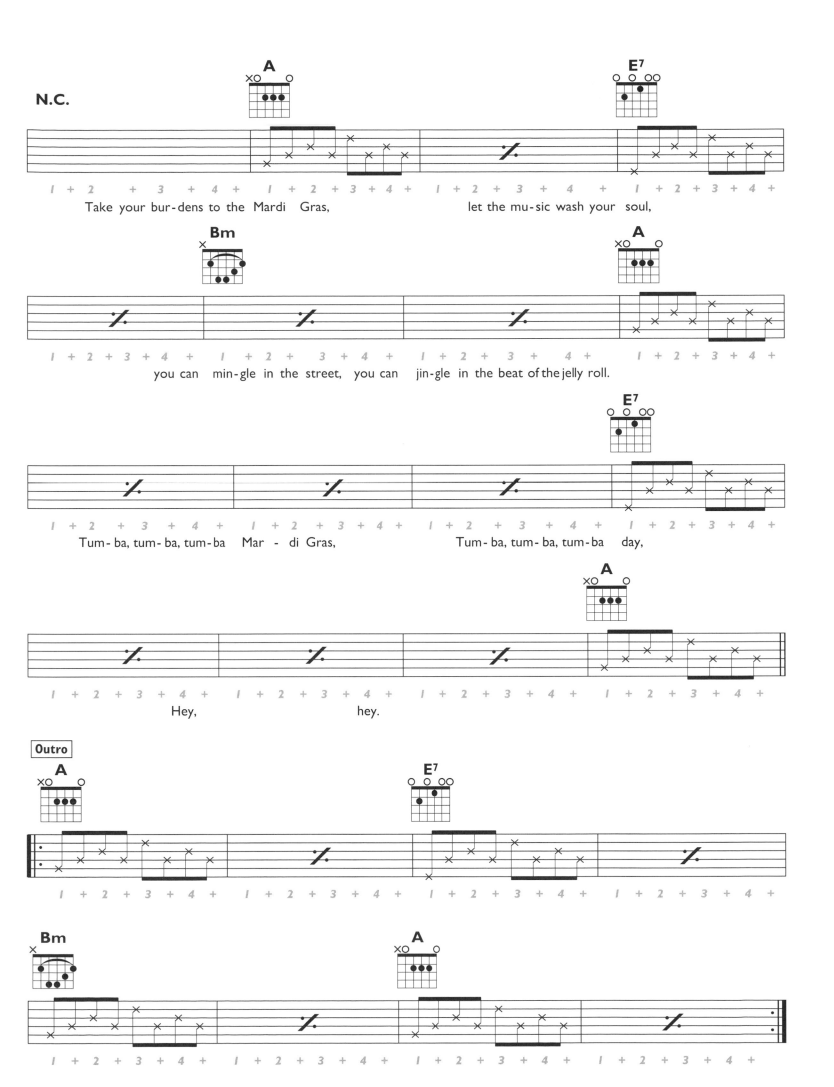

N.C.

Take your bur-dens to the Mardi Gras, let the mu-sic wash your soul,

you can min-gle in the street, you can jin-gle in the beat of the jelly roll.

Tum-ba, tum-ba, tum-ba Mar-di Gras, Tum-ba, tum-ba, tum-ba day,

Hey, hey.

Outro

19

WEDNESDAY MORNING, 3 A.M.
WORDS AND MUSIC BY PAUL SIMON

This song uses combinations of the picking patterns from the previous songs, picking two notes at the start of each bar.

A special system, using the symbols ⊕ and 𝄊, shows the structure of the song. Follow the 𝄆 𝄇 signs and [1. 2.] and [3.] structure as before. However, at the end of the [3.], follow the instruction **Go back to** 𝄊 to take you back to the beginning of the verse. Then look for **Go to** ⊕ to jump to the ⊕ section to end the song.

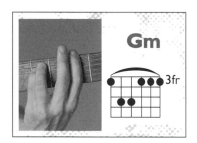

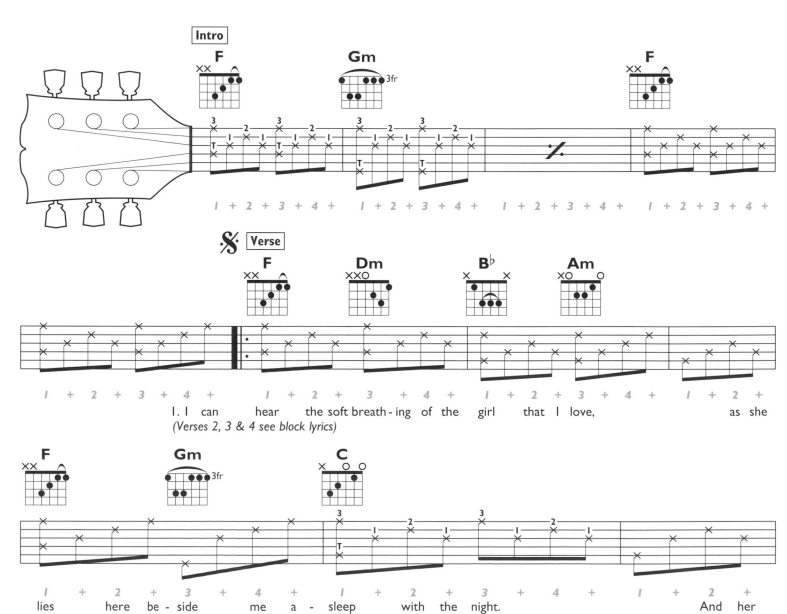

1. I can hear the soft breath-ing of the girl that I love, as she
(Verses 2, 3 & 4 see block lyrics)

lies here be - side me a - sleep with the night. And her

20

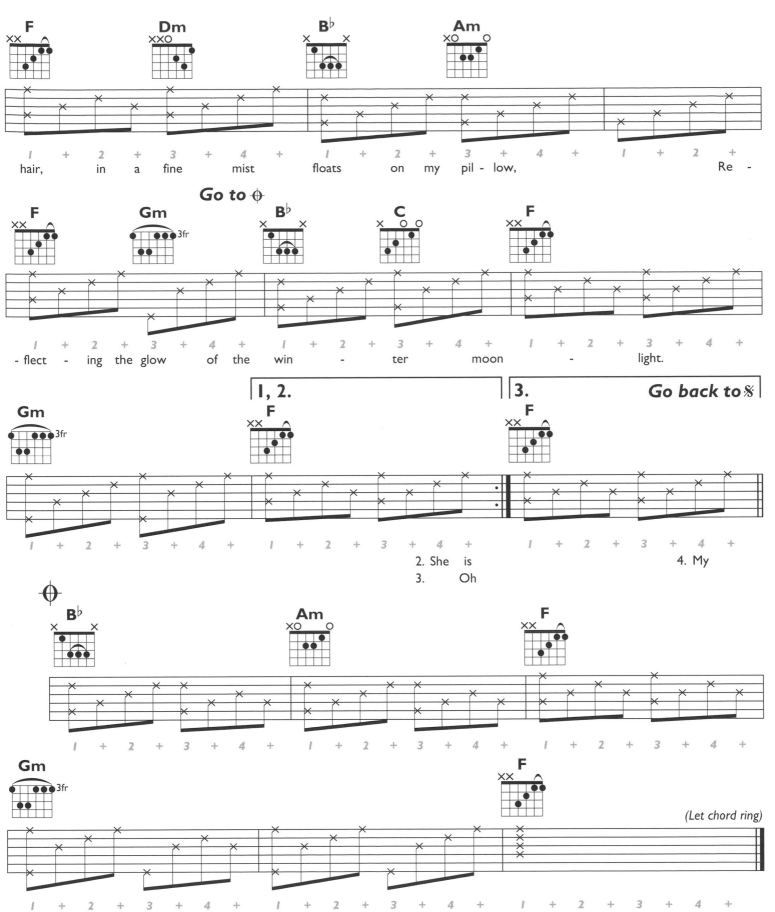

hair, in a fine mist floats on my pil-low, Re -

- flect - ing the glow of the win - ter moon - light.

1, 2.   **3.**   Go back to %

2. She is
3. Oh
4. My

Verse 2:
She is soft, she is warm,
But my heart remains heavy,
And I watch as her breasts
Gently rise, gently fall,
For I know with the first light of dawn
I'll be leaving,
And tonight will be
All I have left to recall.

Verse 3:
Oh, what have I done,
Why have I done it,
I've committed a crime,
I've broken the law.
For twenty-five dollars
And pieces of silver
I held up and robbed
A hard liquor store.

Verse 4:
My life seems unreal,
My crime an illusion,
A scene badly written
In which I must play.
Yet I know as I gaze
At my young love beside me
The morning is just a few hours away.

GRACELAND
WORDS AND MUSIC BY PAUL SIMON

This song has some tricky parts which may take some time to master. The first thing to look out for is the basic groove, where your thumb keeps a strong beat on every other note.

The **F/C** chord is a 'slash' chord. This means that there is a different note under the chord than usual. See how the shape is the similar to the **F** chord in earlier songs, with one additional note, and hear how it contrasts with the main pattern on **C**.

Later in the song there is a rhythm where the beat counts are different, to show that the notes are fast groups of three. Count '*1 + a 2 + a*' when playing these parts; start slowly and then build up to the speed of the song.

Graceland, Elvis Presley's home in Memphis, Tennessee.

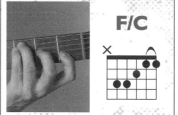

CAPO: 4TH FRET   Intro

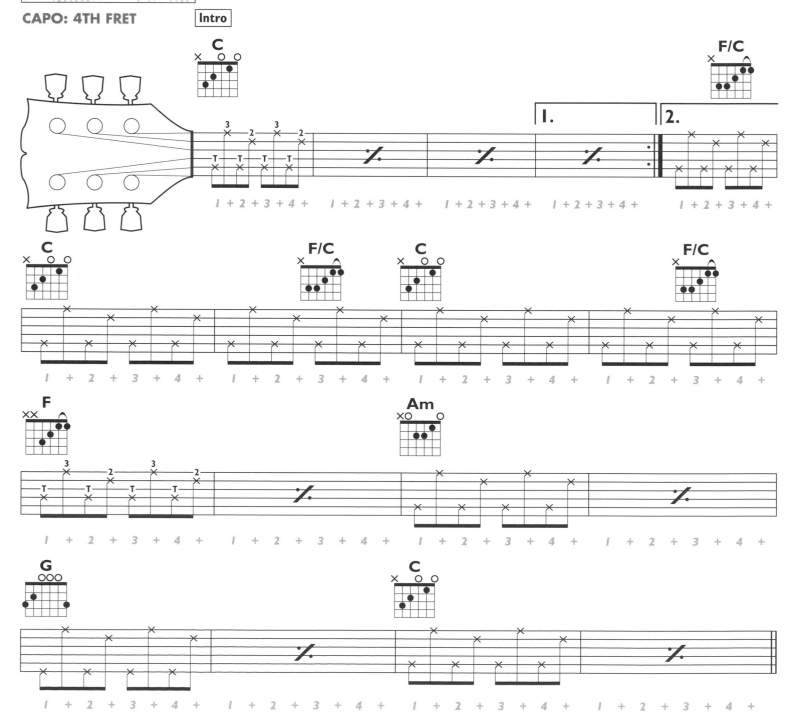

The

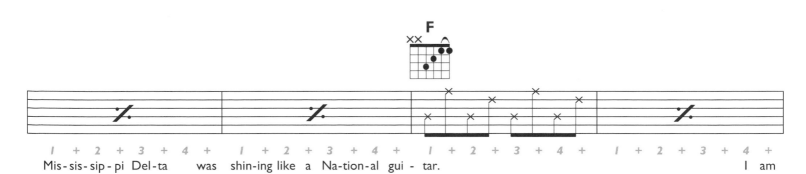

I + 2 + 3 + 4 + I + 2 + 3 + 4 + I + 2 + 3 + 4 + I + 2 + 3 + 4 +

Mis-sis-sip-pi Del-ta was shin-ing like a Na-tion-al gui-tar. I am

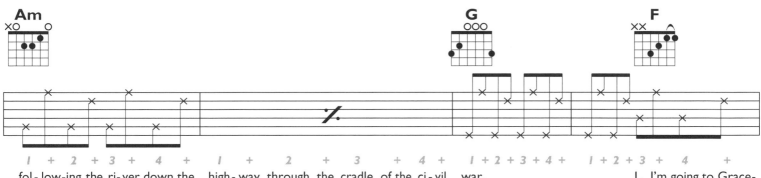

I + 2 + 3 + 4 + I + 2 + 3 + 4 + I + 2 + 3 + 4 + I + 2 + 3 + 4 +

fol-low-ing the ri-ver down the high-way through the cradle of the ci-vil war. 1. I'm going to Grace-

Verse

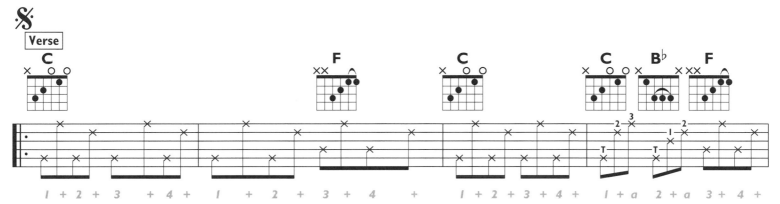

I + 2 + 3 + 4 + I + 2 + 3 + 4 + I + 2 + 3 + 4 + I + a 2 + a 3 + 4 +

-land Grace-land in Mem-phis, Ten-nes-see I'm going to Grace-land.
(Verses 2 & 3 see block lyrics)

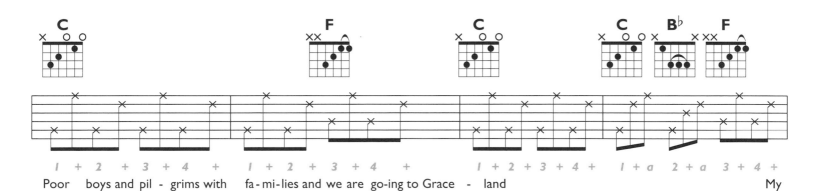

I + 2 + 3 + 4 + I + 2 + 3 + 4 + I + 2 + 3 + 4 + I + a 2 + a 3 + 4 +

Poor boys and pil-grims with fa-mi-lies and we are go-ing to Grace-land My

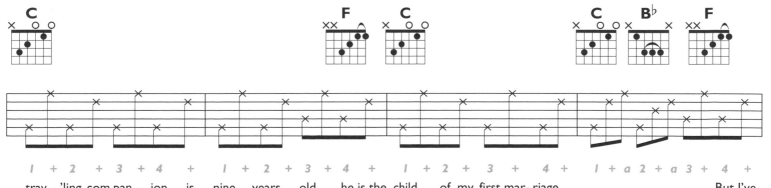

I + 2 + 3 + 4 + I + 2 + 3 + 4 + I + 2 + 3 + 4 + I + a 2 + a 3 + 4 +

trav-'ling com-pan-ion is nine years old he is the child of my first mar-riage. But I've

23

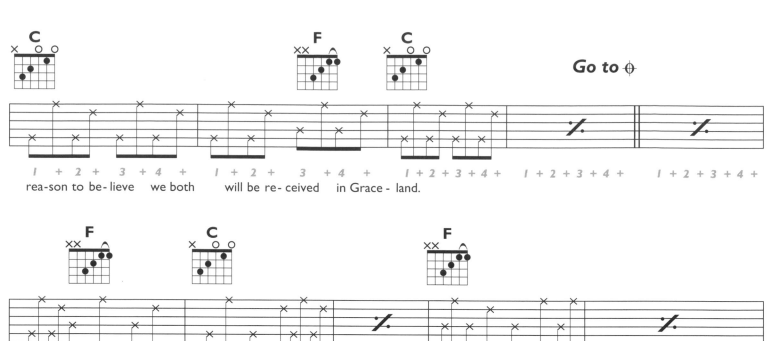

I + 2 + 3 + 4 +   I + 2 + 3 + 4 +   I + 2 + 3 + 4 +   I + 2 + 3 + 4 +   I + 2 + 3 + 4 +

rea-son to be-lieve   we both   will be re-ceived   in Grace-land.

I + 2 + 3   +   4 +   I + 2   + 3 + 4 +   I + 2 + 3 + 4 +   I + 2 + 3   + 4 +   I + 2   + 3   + 4 +

She comes back to   tell me she's gone,   if I did-n't know that as   if I did-n't know my own

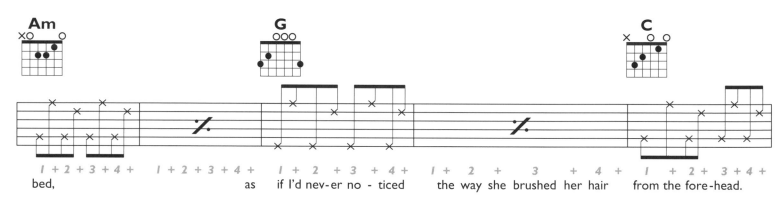

I + 2 + 3 + 4 +   I + 2 + 3 + 4 +   I + 2   + 3   + 4 +   I + 2   + 3   + 4 +   I + 2 + 3 + 4 +

bed,   as   if I'd nev-er no-ticed   the way she brushed her hair   from the fore-head.

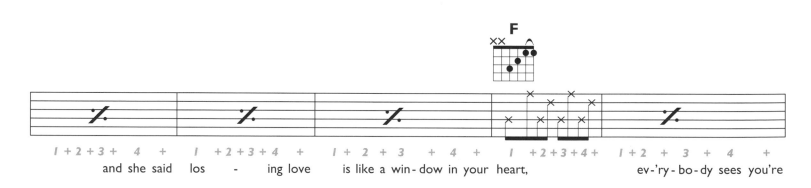

I + 2 + 3 +   4 +   I   + 2 + 3 + 4   +   I + 2 + 3   + 4 +   I   + 2 + 3 + 4 +   I + 2   + 3   + 4 +

and she said los   -   ing love   is like a win-dow in your heart,   ev-'ry-bo-dy sees you're

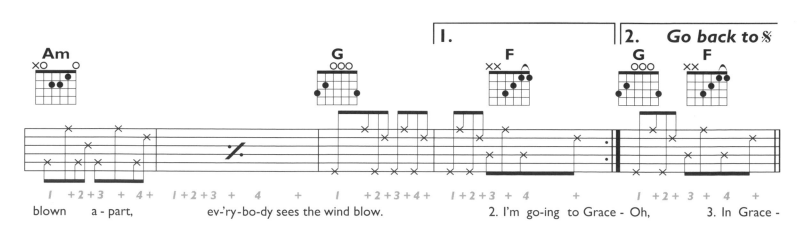

I   + 2 + 3   + 4 +   I + 2 + 3 + 4 +   I   + 2 + 3 + 4 +   I + 2 + 3 + 4   +   I   + 2 + 3   + 4 +

blown   a-part,   ev-'ry-bo-dy sees the wind blow.   2. I'm go-ing to Grace- Oh,   3. In Grace-

24

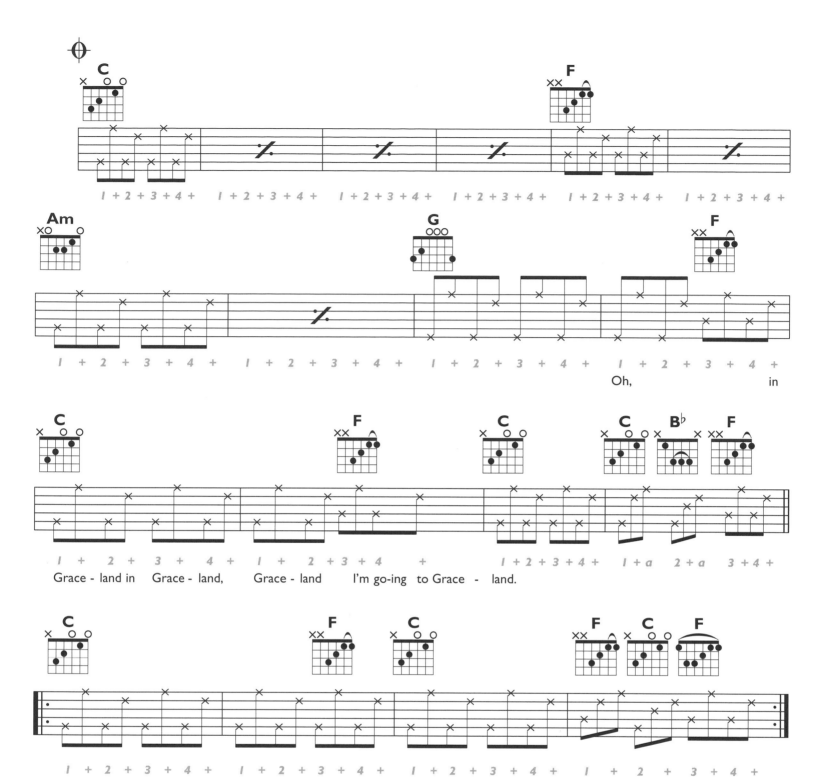

THE 59TH STREET BRIDGE SONG (FEELIN' GROOVY)

WORDS AND MUSIC BY PAUL SIMON

The 59th Street Bridge, New York City.

This song is different from the rest of the book; instead of a steady picking rhythm, you play a 'riff' which repeats throughout the song. This riff is only two bars long, so that's all you need to learn to play the whole song. Note that it doesn't start on the first beat! Follow the rhythm counts carefully.

CAPO: 1ST FRET

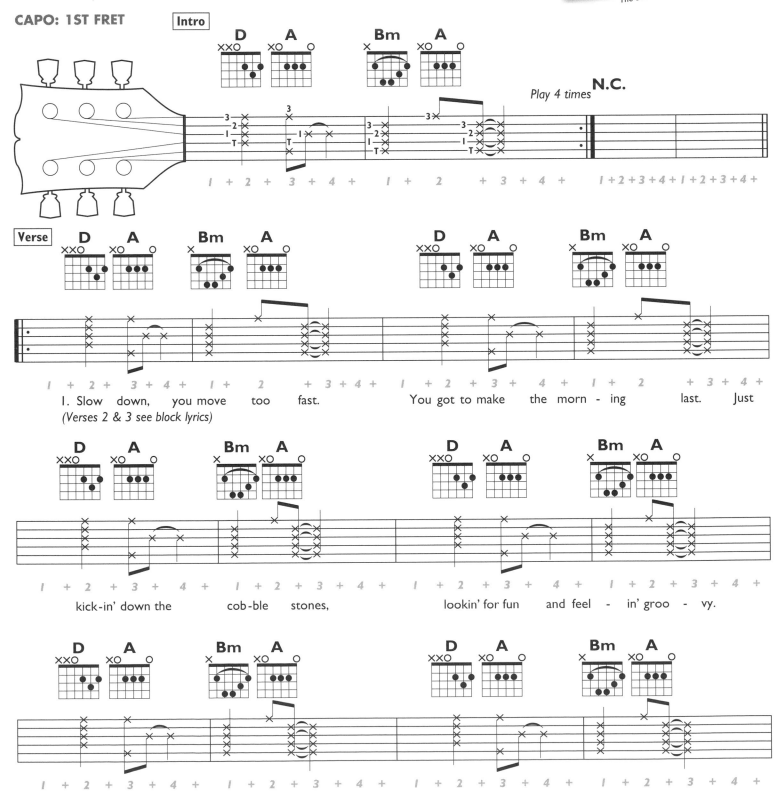

1. Slow down, you move too fast. You got to make the morn - ing last. Just
(Verses 2 & 3 see block lyrics)

kick-in' down the cob-ble stones, lookin' for fun and feel - in' groo - vy.

Ba da da da da da da feel - in' groo - vy.

26

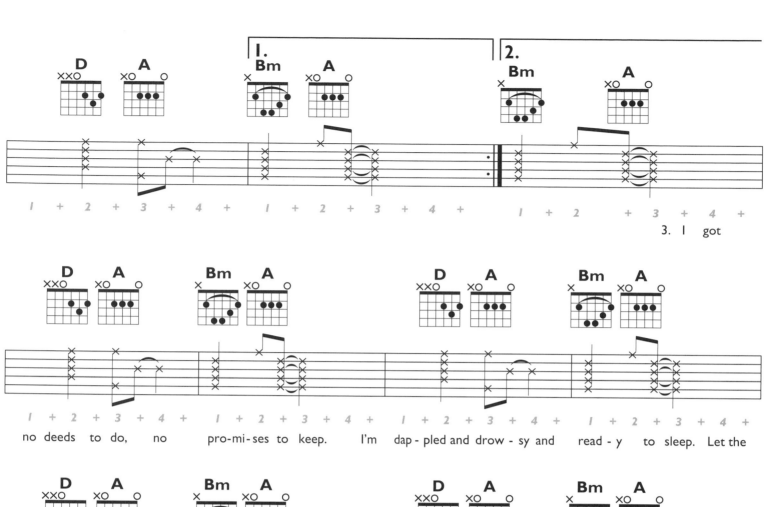

3. I got

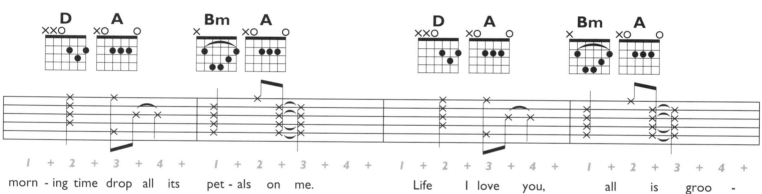

no deeds to do, no pro-mi-ses to keep. I'm dap-pled and drow-sy and read-y to sleep. Let the

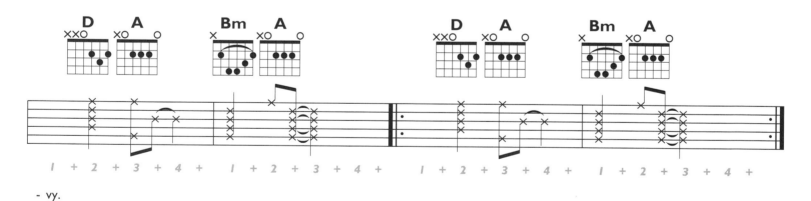

morn-ing time drop all its pet-als on me. Life I love you, all is groo -

- vy.

Verse 2:
Hello lamp-post,
What cha knowin'?
I've come to watch your flowers growin'.
Ain't cha got no rhymes for me?
Doot-in' doo-doo,
Feelin' groovy.

Verse 3:
I got no deeds to do,
No promises to keep.
I'm dappled and drowsy and ready to sleep.
Let the morning time drop all its petals on me.
Life, I love you,
All is groovy.

MRS. ROBINSON
WORDS AND MUSIC BY PAUL SIMON

The picking pattern for this song is really fast! Start slowly, and steadily build up speed. The **E⁷** shape for this song is slightly different to the one shown previously, adding another finger. The picking pattern for this chord alternates your thumb on the two lowest strings. This song also has a ⊕ structure; remember that you only **Go to** ⊕ on the last time through the verse.

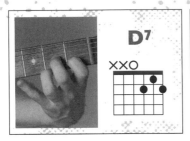

Several Paul Simon songs, including this one, were featured on the soundtrack to Mike Nichols' 1967 film The Graduate, starring Dustin Hoffman and Anne Bancroft, above.

CAPO: 2ND FRET

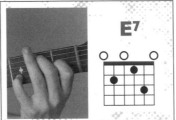

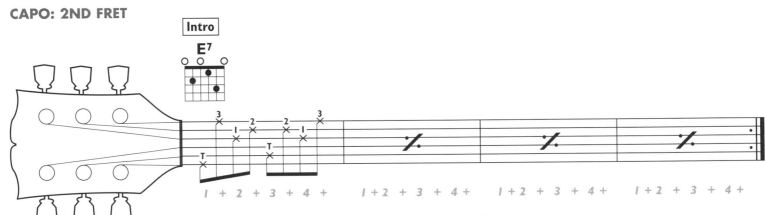

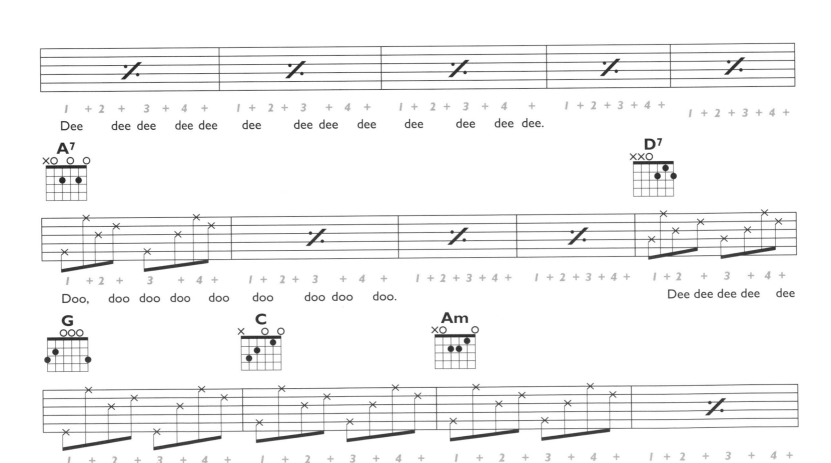

28

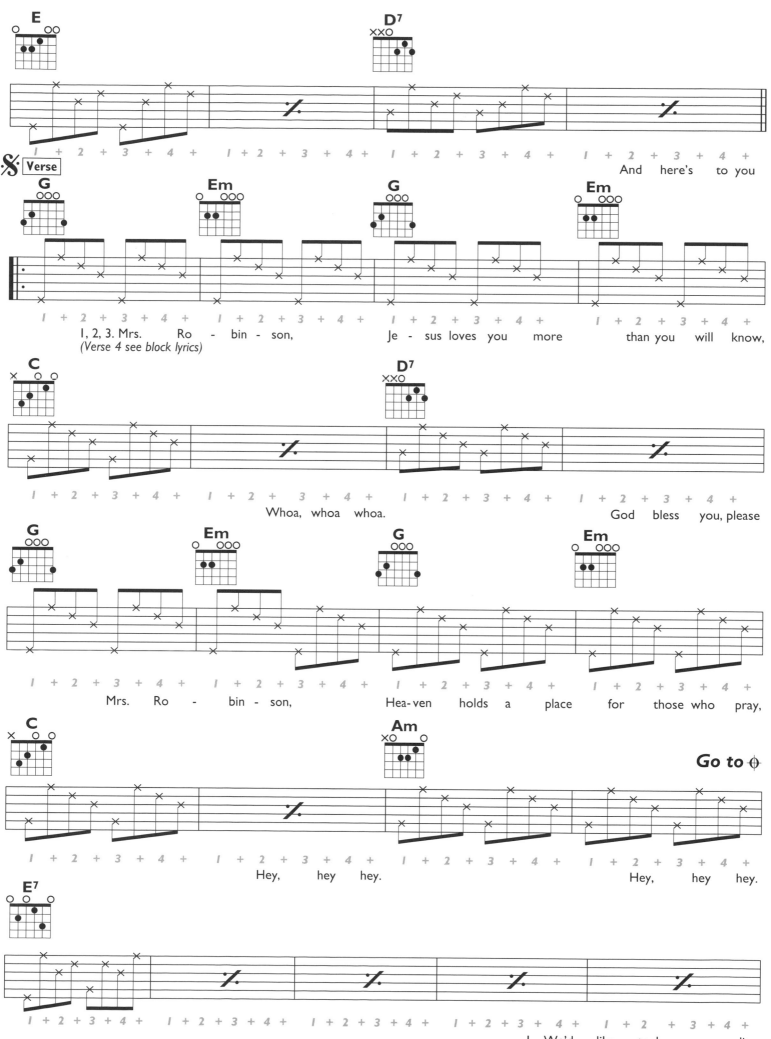

29

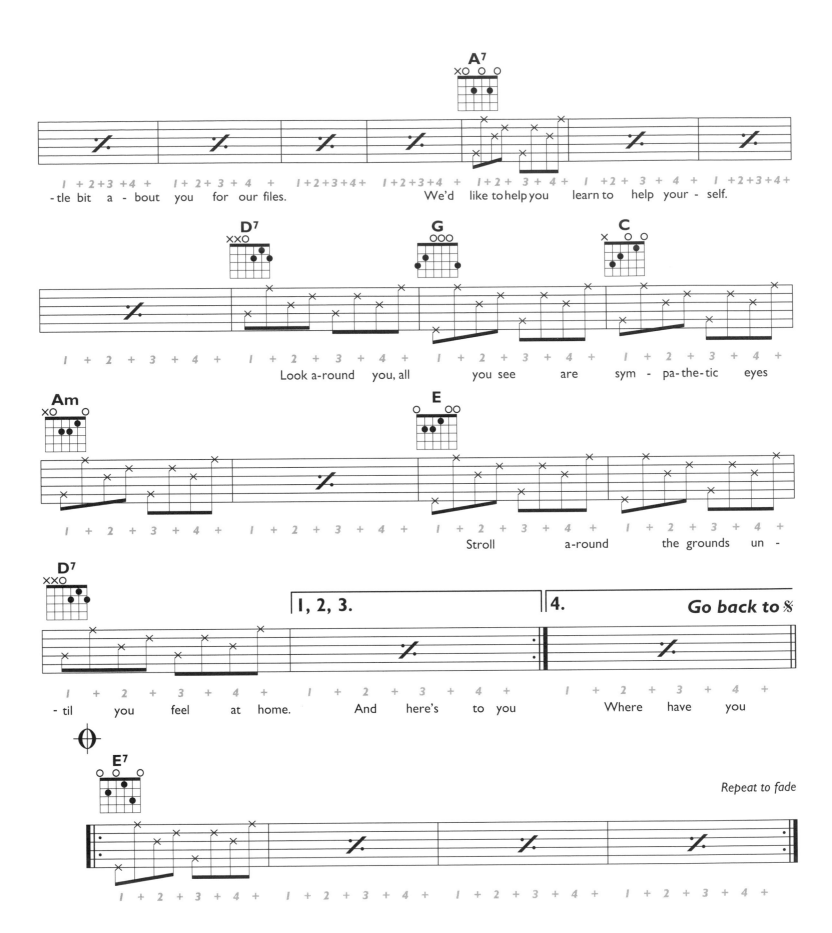

Verse 2:
Hide it in a hiding place where no one ever goes,
Put it in your pantry with your cupcakes.
It's a little secret, just the Robinson's affair
Most of all, you've got to hide it from the kids
Coo, coo ca-choo.

Verse 3:
Sitting on a sofa on a Sunday afternoon,
Going to the candidates' debate,
Laught about it, shout about it,
When you've got to choose,
Every way you look at it you lose.

Verse 4:
Where have you gone, Joe DiMaggio?
A nation turns its lonely eyes to you.
Woo, woo, woo.
What's that you say, Mrs. Robinson?
"Joltin' Joe has left and gone away."
Hey, hey, hey, hey, hey, hey.

HOMEWARD BOUND
WORDS AND MUSIC BY PAUL SIMON

Homeward bound...

This song has three new barre chord shapes: **C♯m/G♯**, **Em⁶/G** and **F♯7**. Practice repeating the first eight bars of the verse until you can switch between these smoothly. The chorus features quick changes between **Bm**, **A**, **G** and **D**, picking each chord in full. Look carefully at the crosses on the strings to see which strings to pick.

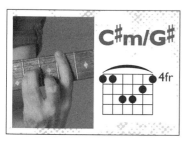

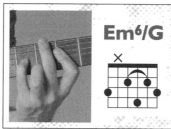

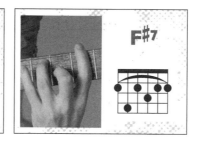

CAPO: 1ST FRET

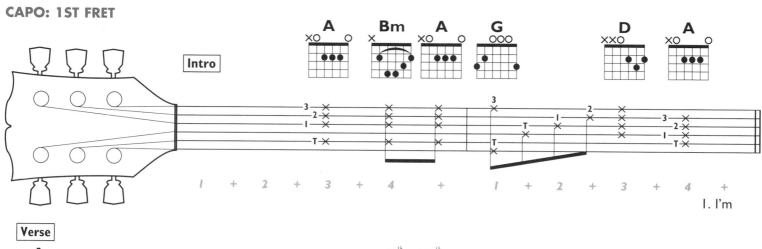

Verse

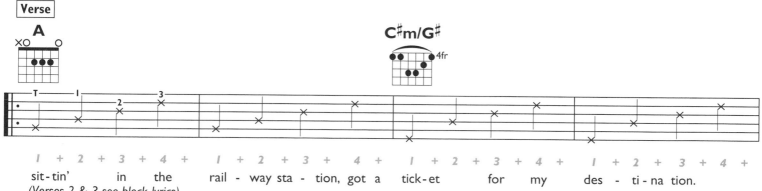

sit - tin' in the rail - way sta - tion, got a tick - et for my des - ti - na tion.
(Verses 2 & 3 see block lyrics)

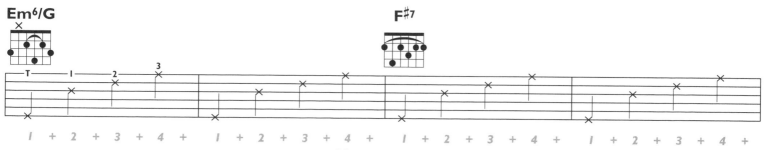

Mm.

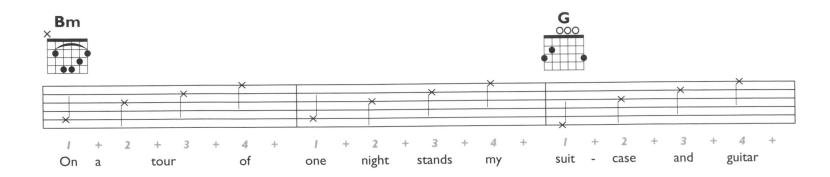

Bm   **G**

1 + 2 + 3 + 4 + | 1 + 2 + 3 + 4 + | 1 + 2 + 3 + 4 +

On a   tour   of   one   night   stands   my   suit - case   and   guitar

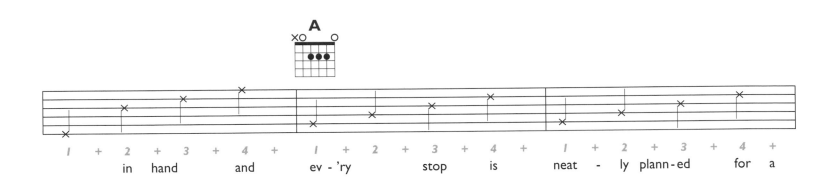

A

1 + 2 + 3 + 4 + | 1 + 2 + 3 + 4 + | 1 + 2 + 3 + 4 +

in   hand   and   ev - 'ry   stop   is   neat - ly   plann-ed   for a

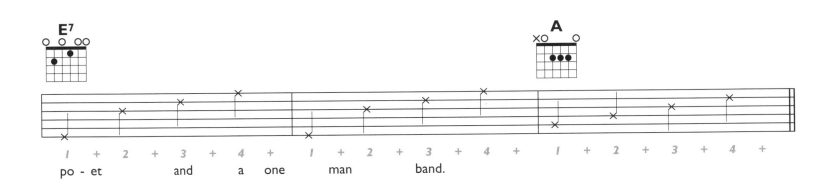

E⁷   **A**

1 + 2 + 3 + 4 + | 1 + 2 + 3 + 4 + | 1 + 2 + 3 + 4 +

po - et   and   a   one   man   band.

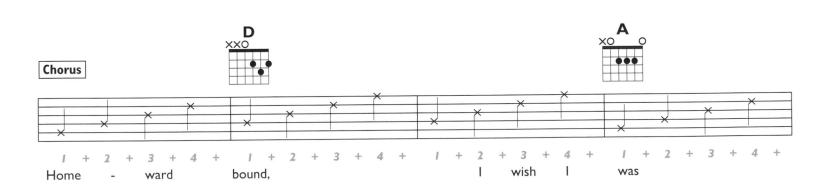

Chorus   **D**   **A**

1 + 2 + 3 + 4 + | 1 + 2 + 3 + 4 + | 1 + 2 + 3 + 4 + | 1 + 2 + 3 + 4 +

Home - ward   bound,   I   wish   I   was

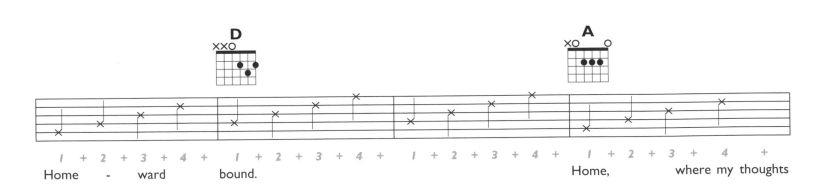

D   **A**

1 + 2 + 3 + 4 + | 1 + 2 + 3 + 4 + | 1 + 2 + 3 + 4 + | 1 + 2 + 3 + 4 +

Home - ward   bound.   Home,   where my thoughts

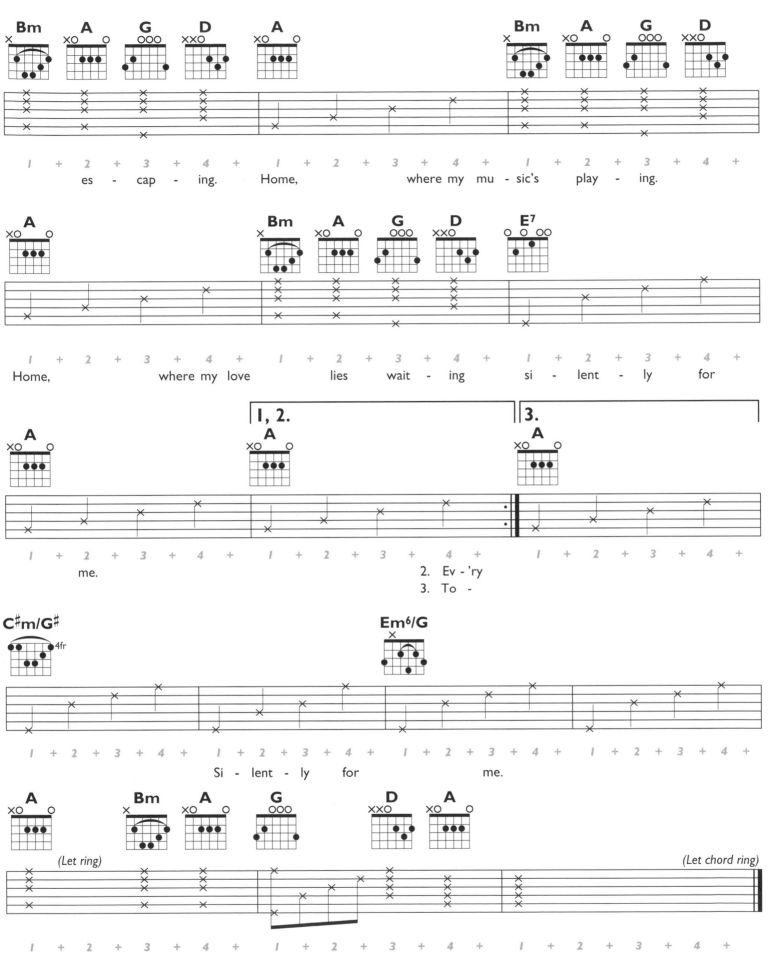

Verse 2:
Everyday's an endless stream
Of cigarettes and magazines.
And each town looks the same to me,
The movies and the factories,
And every stranger's face I see
Reminds me that I long to be...

Verse 3:
Tonight I'll sing my songs again,
I'll play the game and pretend.
But all my words come back to me
In shades of mediocrity,
Like emptiness in harmony.
I need someone to comfort me.

FIFTY WAYS TO LEAVE YOUR LOVER
WORDS AND MUSIC BY PAUL SIMON

This song has lots of new chords, with complicated sounding names, but don't be put off! The song is quite slow, and most of the shapes should fall under the fingers quite easily with a little practice. The jazzy, sophisticated sound will then come across. In the verses, pick each chord and let it ring, moving between each chord to follow the melody. The chorus should have a lot more energy and a steady fingerpicking pattern.

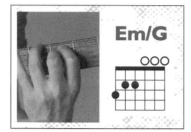

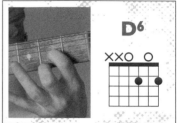

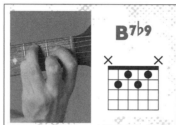

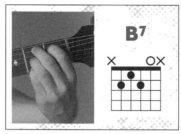

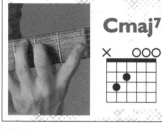

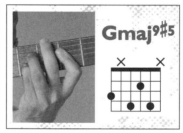

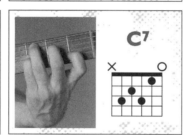

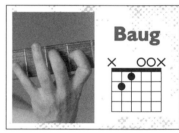

Verse

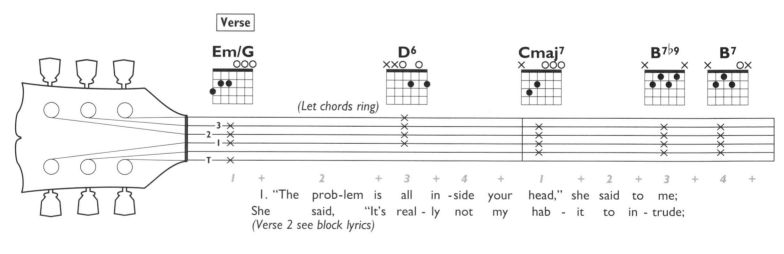

(Let chords ring)

1. "The prob-lem is all in-side your head," she said to me;
She said, "It's real-ly not my hab-it to in-trude;
(Verse 2 see block lyrics)

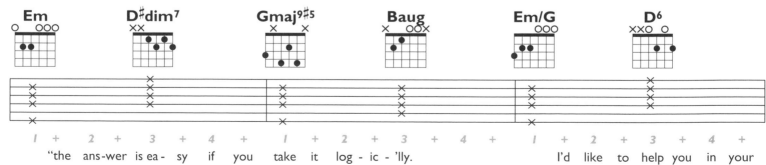

"the ans-wer is ea-sy if you take it log-ic-'lly.
I hope my mean-ing won't be lost or mis-con-strued.

I'd like to help you in your
But I'll re-peat my-self at the

34

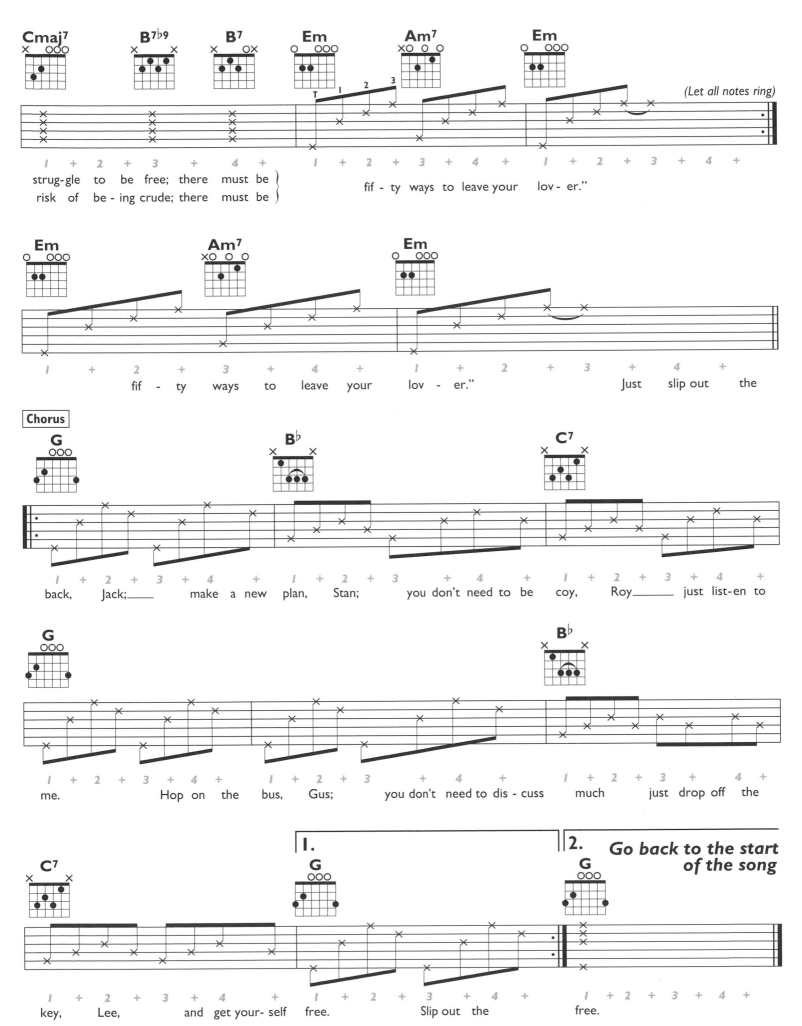

Verse 2:

She said, "It grieves me so to see you in such pain;
I wish there was something I could do to make you smile again."
I said, "I appreciate that, and would you please explain about the fifty ways?"

She said, "Why don't we both just sleep on it tonight;
And I believe in the morning you'll begin to see the light."
And then she kissed me and I realized she was probably right;
There must be fifty ways to leave your lover.

THAT'S WHERE I BELONG

WORDS AND MUSIC BY PAUL SIMON

There are some new chords for this song; most of them are similar to chords used earlier in the book (compare **Bm** to **Bm⁷**, for instance).

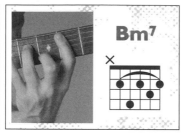

CAPO: 1ST FRET

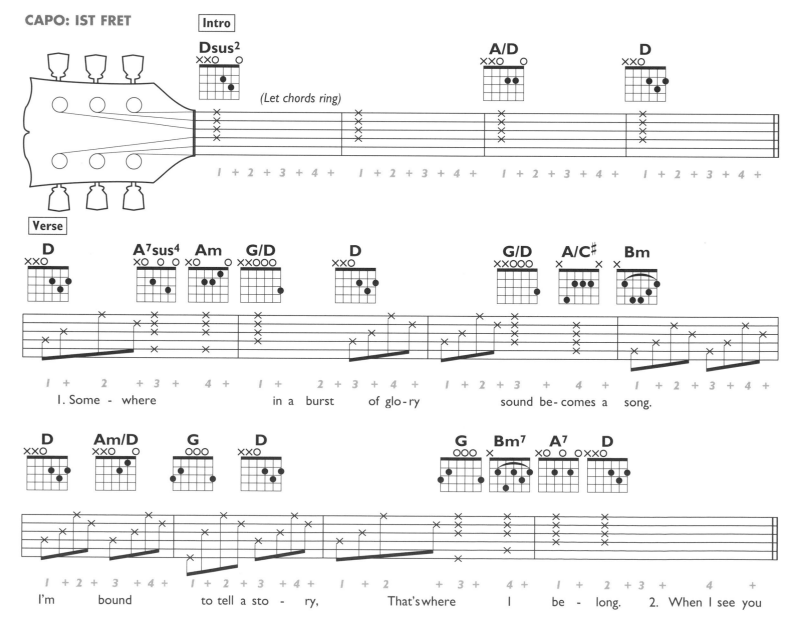

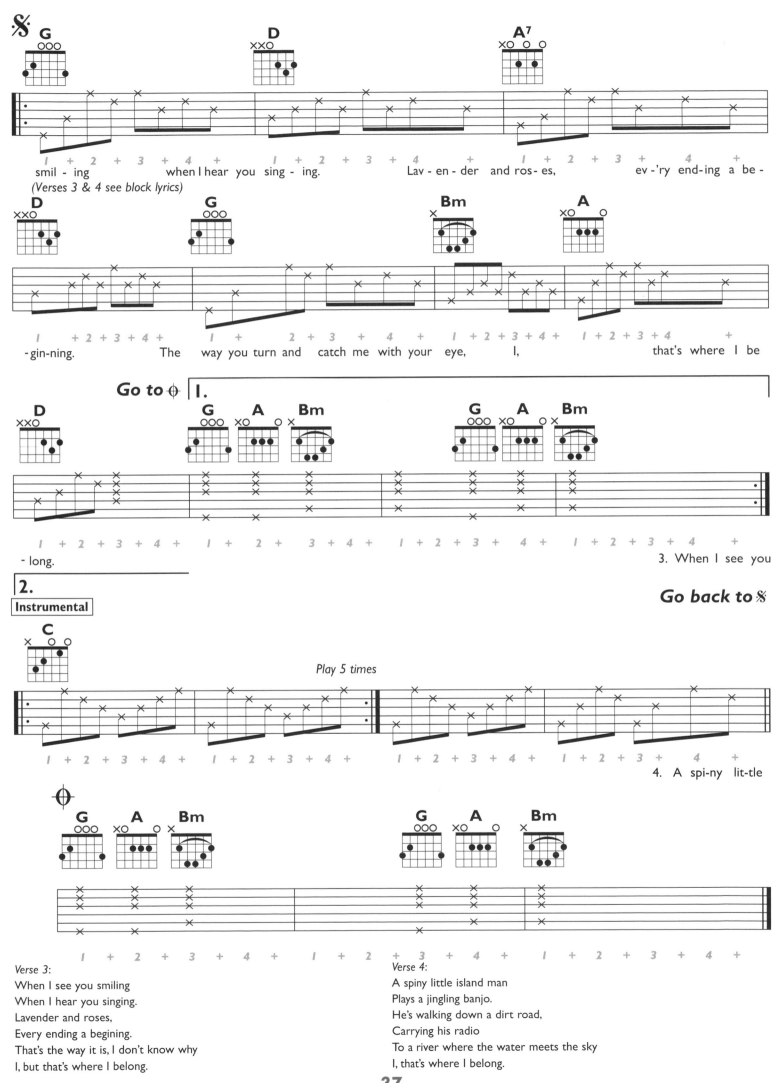

Verse 3:
When I see you smiling
When I hear you singing.
Lavender and roses,
Every ending a begining.
That's the way it is, I don't know why
I, but that's where I belong.

Verse 4:
A spiny little island man
Plays a jingling banjo.
He's walking down a dirt road,
Carrying his radio
To a river where the water meets the sky
I, that's where I belong.

KATHY'S SONG
WORDS AND MUSIC BY PAUL SIMON

The opening chord of this song has quite a mysterious sound. To match the recording, you'll have to tune the guitar down a half-step (or semitone), so that the lowest string is E^b rather than E.

Moving between G and C/G is easiest if you finger the G chord as shown in the box below.

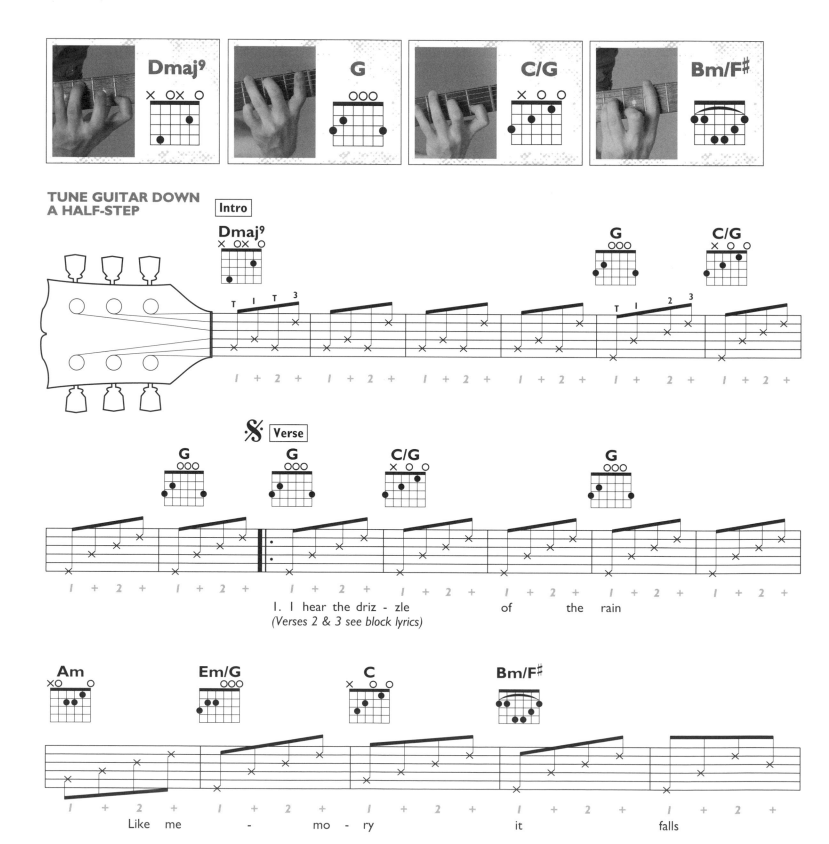

TUNE GUITAR DOWN A HALF-STEP

1. I hear the driz - zle of the rain
(Verses 2 & 3 see block lyrics)

Like me - mo - ry it falls

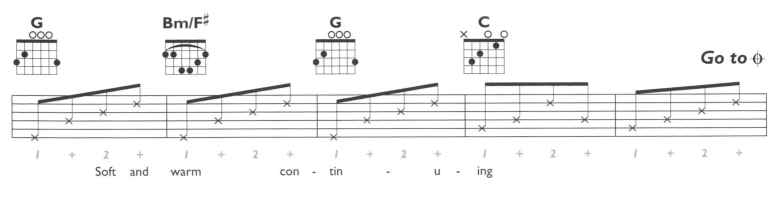

Soft and warm con - tin - u - ing

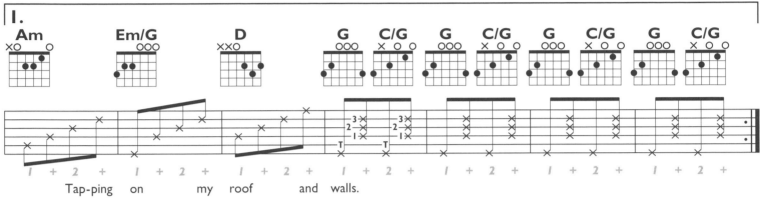

Tap-ping on my roof and walls.

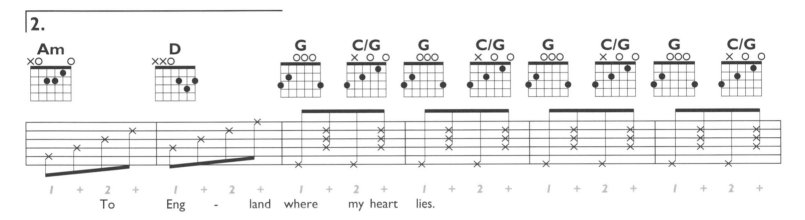

To Eng - land where my heart lies.

Go back to %

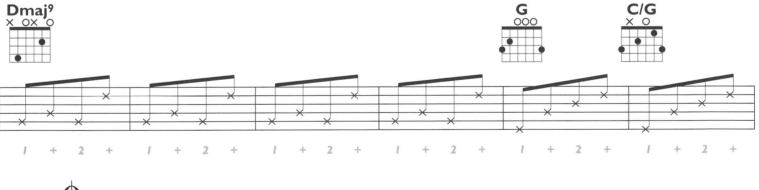

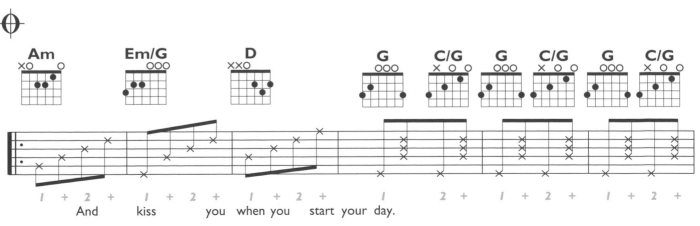

And kiss you when you start your day.

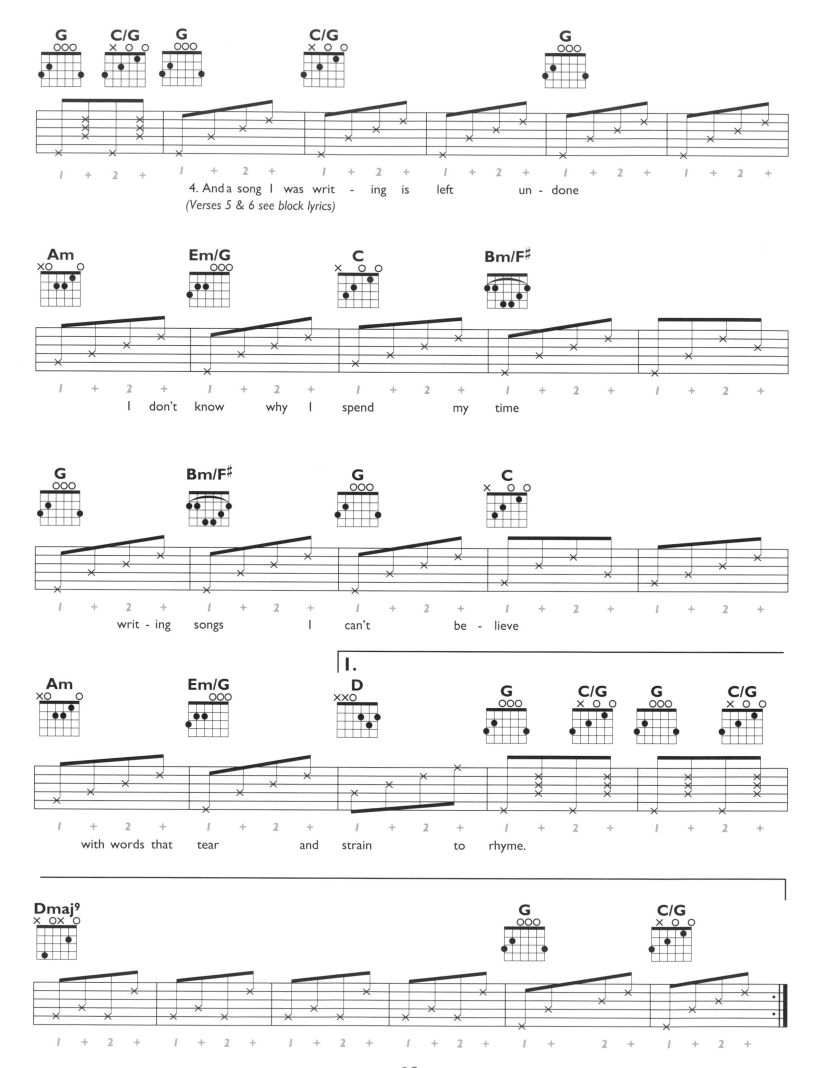

4. And a song I was writ - ing is left un - done
(Verses 5 & 6 see block lyrics)

I don't know why I spend my time

writ - ing songs I can't be - lieve

with words that tear and strain to rhyme.

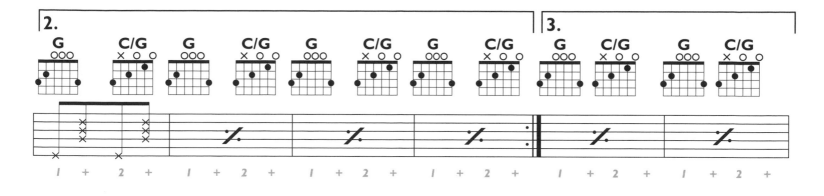

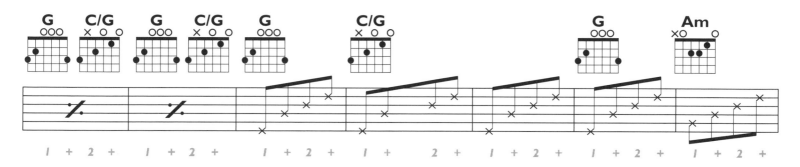

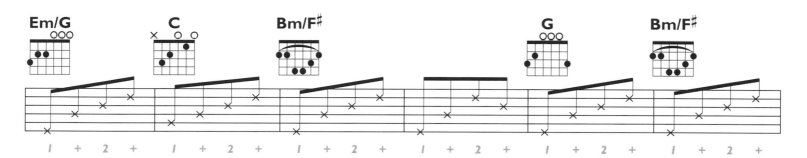

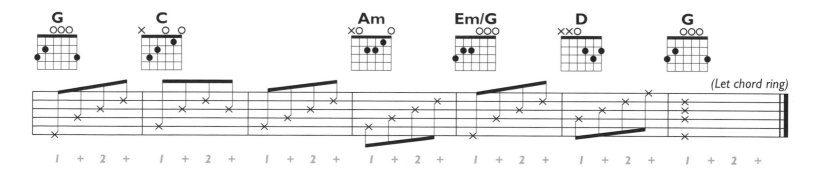

Verse 2:
And from the shelter of my mind
Through the window of my eyes
I gaze beyound the rain-drenched streets
To England where my heart lies.

Verse 3:
My mind's distracted and diffused
My thoughts are many miles away
They lie with you when you're asleep
And kiss you when you start your day.

Verse 5:
And so you see I have come to doubt
All that I once held as true
I stand alone without beliefs
The only truth I know is you.

Verse 6:
And as I watch the drops of rain
Weave their weary paths and die
I know that I am like the rain
There but for the grace of you go I.

AMERICA
WORDS AND MUSIC BY PAUL SIMON

This song has six counts in each bar. The thumbed notes in the opening sequence create a bass line, linking the chords together.

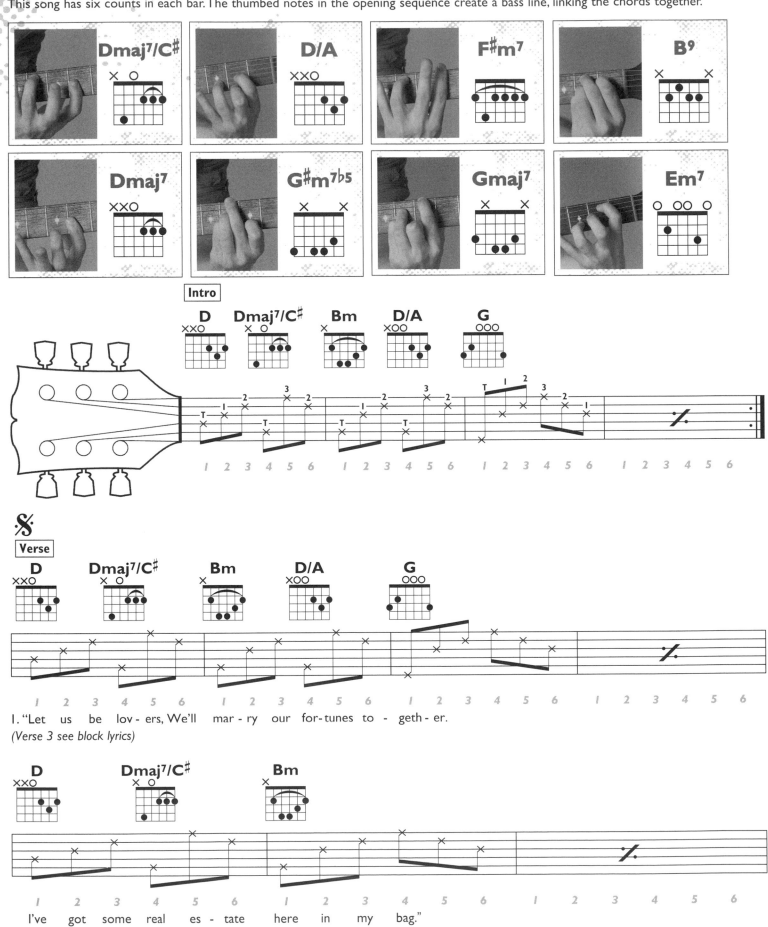

1. "Let us be lov - ers, We'll mar - ry our for-tunes to - geth - er.
(Verse 3 see block lyrics)

I've got some real es - tate here in my bag."

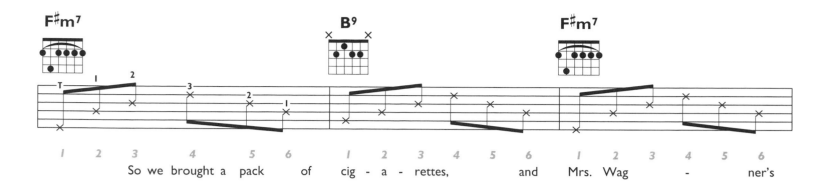

So we brought a pack of cig - a - rettes, and Mrs. Wag - - ner's

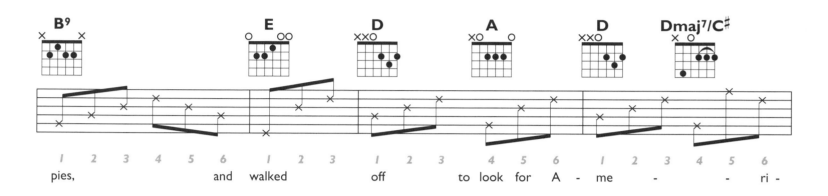

pies, and walked off to look for A - me - - ri -

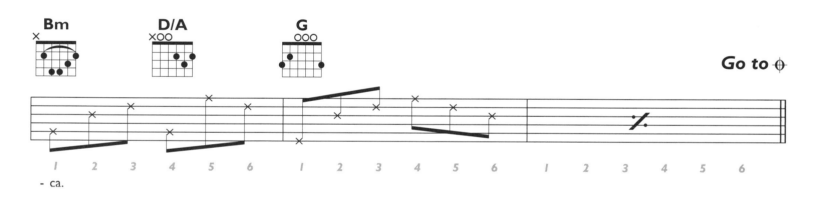

Go to ⊕

- ca.

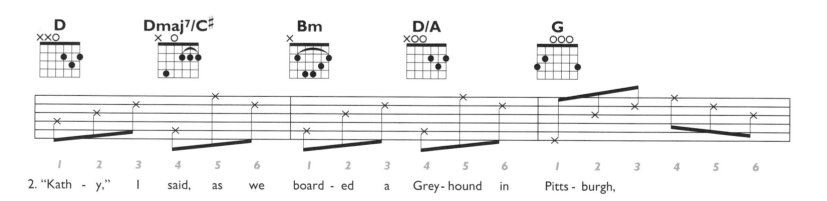

2. "Kath - y," I said, as we board - ed a Grey - hound in Pitts - burgh,

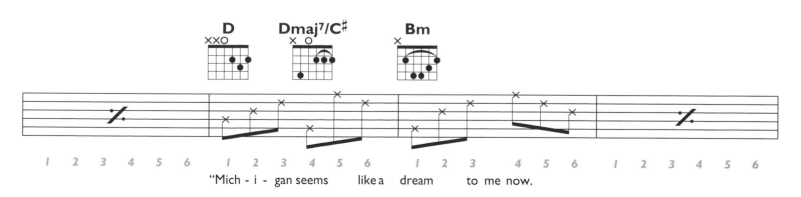

"Mich - i - gan seems like a dream to me now.

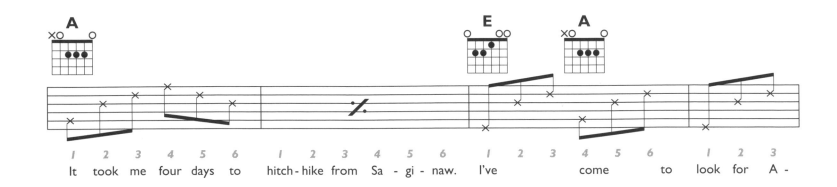

It took me four days to hitch-hike from Sa - gi - naw. I've come to look for A -

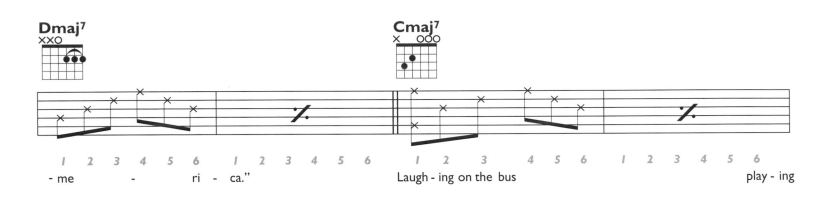

- me - ri - ca." Laugh - ing on the bus playing

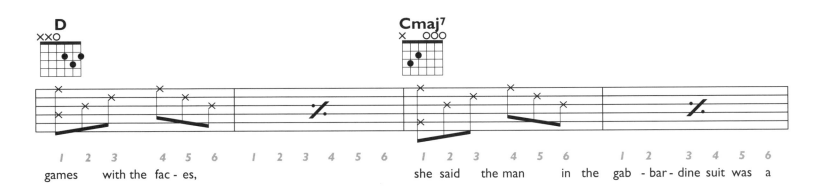

games with the fac - es, she said the man in the gab - bar - dine suit was a

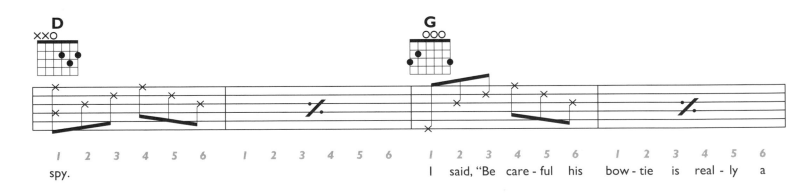

spy. I said, "Be care - ful his bow - tie is real - ly a

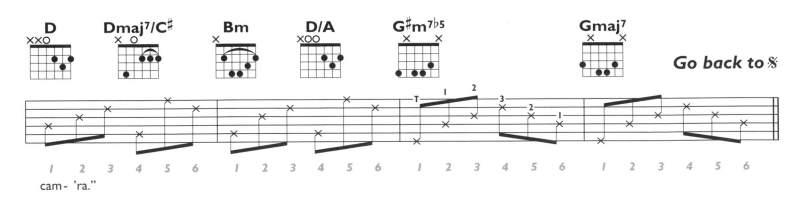

Go back to ⅌

cam - 'ra."

4. "Kath-y, I'm lost," I said, though I knew she was sleep-ing. "I'm

emp-ty and ach-ing and I don't know why." Count-ing the cars on the

New Jer-sey Turn-pike. They've all come to look for A - me - ri - ca.

All come to look for A - me - ri - ca.

Repeat to fade

Verse 3:
"Toss me a cigarette, I think there's one in my raincoat."
"We smoked the last one an hour ago."
So I looked at the scenery, she read her magazine;
And the moon rose over an open field.

AMERICAN TUNE
WORDS AND MUSIC BY PAUL SIMON

Look out for the changing patterns of rhythm counts in this song. Some of the bars have four counts, some have three, and some have two. Check the crosses on the strings carefully; sometimes you won't be playing the lowest-sounding note of the chord shown in the chord box. This is to create smooth progressions from one chord to the next.

A replica of The Mayflower, that brought the pilgrims to the New World in 1620.

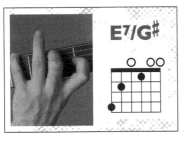

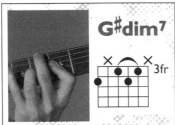

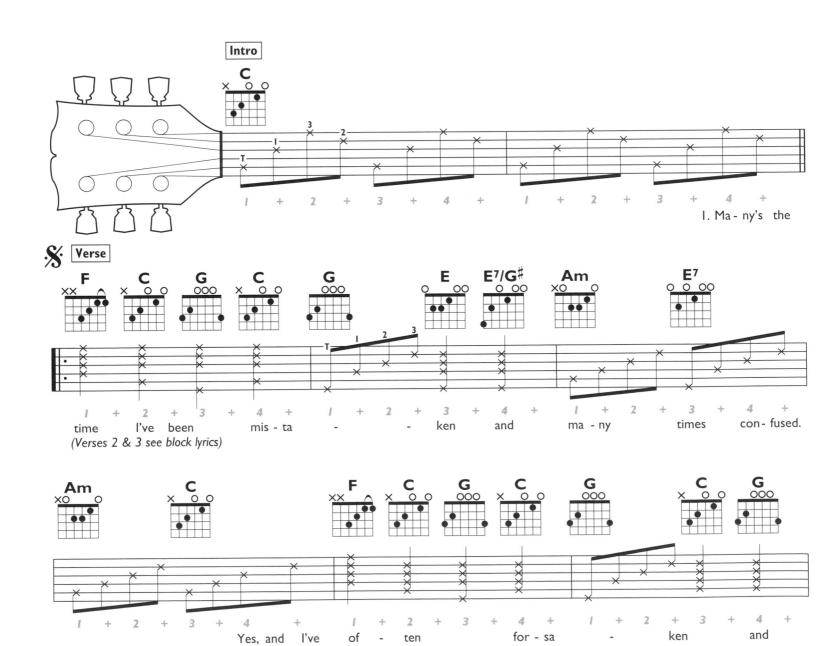

1. Ma - ny's the

time I've been mis - ta - - ken and ma - ny times con - fused.

(Verses 2 & 3 see block lyrics)

Yes, and I've of - ten for - sa - ken and

46

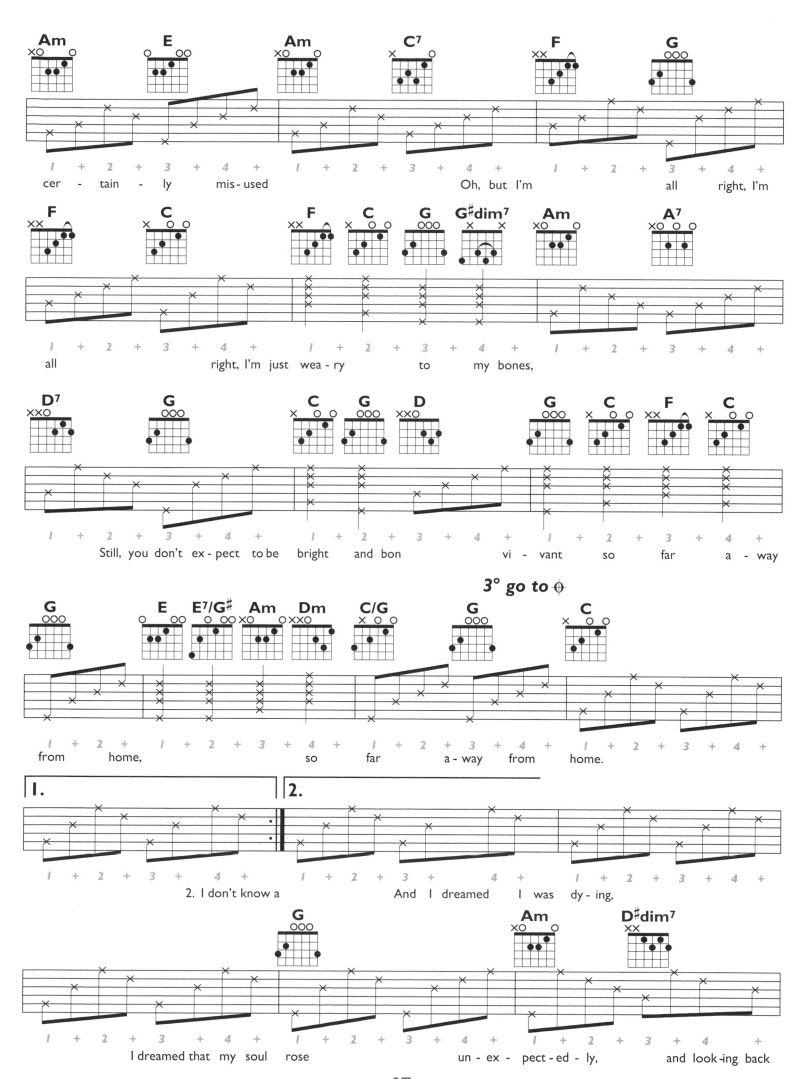

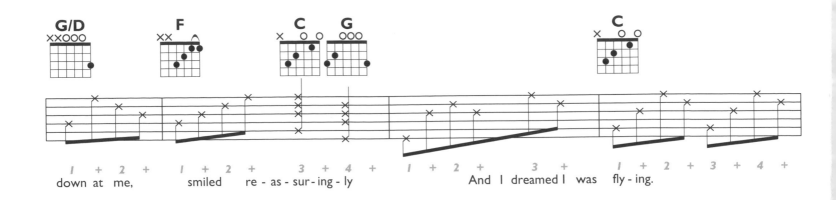

1 + 2 +   1 + 2 +   3 + 4 +   1 + 2 +   3 +   1 + 2 + 3 + 4 +

down at me,   smiled   re - as - sur-ing - ly   And I dreamed I was   fly - ing.

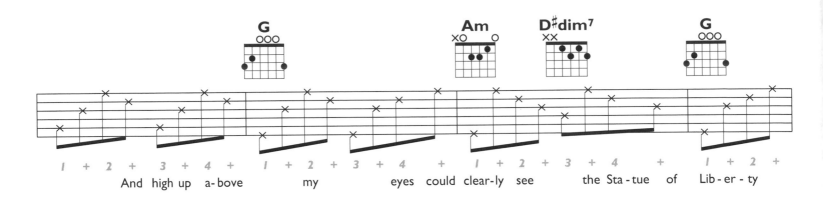

1 + 2 + 3 + 4 +   1 + 2 + 3 + 4 +   1 + 2 + 3 + 4 +   1 + 2 +

And high up a-bove   my   eyes could clear-ly see   the Sta-tue of Lib-er-ty

Go back to 𝄋

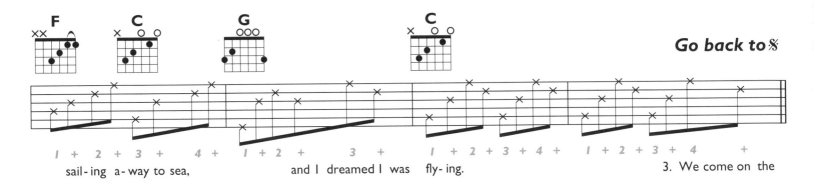

1 + 2 + 3 + 4 +   1 + 2 + 3 +   1 + 2 + 3 + 4 +   1 + 2 + 3 + 4 +   +

sail-ing a-way to sea,   and I dreamed I was   fly-ing.   3. We come on the

(Let chord ring)

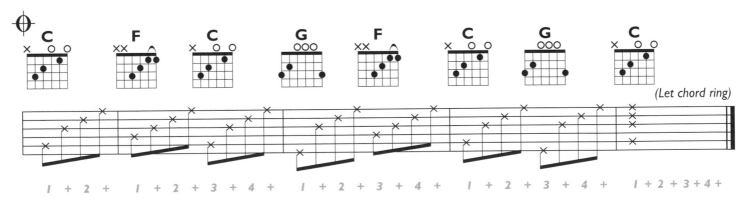

1 + 2 +   1 + 2 + 3 + 4 +   1 + 2 + 3 + 4 +   1 + 2 + 3 + 4 +   1 + 2 + 3 + 4 +

Verse 2:
I don't know a soul who's not been battered,
I don't have a friend who feels at ease.
I don't know a dream that's not been shattered
Or driven to its knees.
But it's all right, it's all right,
We've lived so well so long.
Still, when I think of the road we're traveling on
I wonder what's gone wrong.
I can't help it, I wonder what's gone wrong.

Verse 3:
We come on the ship they call the Mayflower,
We come on the ship that sailed the moon.
We come in the age's most uncertain hours
And sing an American tune,
Oh, and it's alright, it's all right, it's all right.
You can't be forever blessed.
Still, tomorrow's goin' to be another working day,
And I'm trying to get some rest,
That's all, I'm trying to get some rest.

1 2 3 4 5 6 7 8 9